2 000564050 3C

GW00994383

CLL

		15. 11. 7.	
-9. JUL. 1975	07. FEB 77		
18. AUG. 1975	05. MAR 77		
-4. SEP. 1975	13. APR 17 OCT 1977		
30. SEP. 1975			
28. OCT. 1975	12. OCT 77		
-3. JAN. 1976 19. FEB. 1976			
26. MAR 76 22 APR 1976			

WITHDRAWN FROM THE ROTHERHAM PUBLIC LIBRARY

ROTHERHAM PUBLIC LIBRARIES

This book must be returned by the latest date entered above.

The loan may be extended (personally, by post or telephone) for a further period if the book is not required by another reader.

LM 1

China
Tea Clippers

Sir Lancelot

George F. Campbell
Drawings by the author

China
Tea Clippers

Adlard Coles Limited
London

Granada Publishing Limited
First published in Great Britain by Adlard Coles Limited
Frogmore St Albans Hertfordshire AL2 2NF and
3 Upper James Street London W1R 4BP

Copyright © 1974 George F. Campbell

All rights reserved. No part of this publication may be
reproduced, stored in a retrieval system, or transmitted,
in any form or by any means, electronic, mechanical, photocopying,
recording or otherwise, without the prior permission
of the publisher

ISBN 0 229 11525 X *PN 56405*

Printed in Great Britain by
William Clowes & Sons, Limited
London, Beccles and Colchester

ROTHERHAM
PUBLIC LIBRARY

623.822   *HX*

6127-2

LAST COPY
DO NOT WITHDRAW

To my first and last mate, Peggy

Contents

Illustrations

Chapter One

The best of Queens and best of herbs we owe
To that bold nation which the way did show
To the fair region where the sun does rise,
Whose rich productions we so justly prize.
The Muses' friend, Tea, does our fancy aid;
Repress those vapours which the head invade;
And keeps that palace of the soul serene,
Fit on her birthday to salute the Queen.

The Background to the Tea Trade

Thus wrote the poet Waller on the occasion of a birthday to Catherine, the wife of Charles II, the 'bold nation' being the Dutch. Catherine (of Braganza) had brought the habit of tea drinking with her from Portugal and had popularized it at Court, the Portuguese having acquired the taste through their depot at Macao, established in 1557. Tea was something of a curiosity with supposed medicinal powers, and was extremely expensive.

The Dutch East India Company shipped it first to Holland via Java, and it was then transhipped to London, the first merchant selling it there in 1657. When the London East India Company wished to make a present of it to Charles II in 1664, they were able to procure only 2 lbs 2 oz, for which they had to pay eighty-five shillings. Prices at this period reached to one hundred and one hundred and twenty shillings a pound.

The London East India Company, also known as the Honourable Company or John Company, decided to purchase direct from China themselves, and in 1689 made their first shipment from Amoy. The export trade from England was chiefly in lead, tin and wool, to China via India, where opium was also added to the cargo. The Company, by virtue of Cromwell's Navigation Act of 1651, had a monopoly of the Indian Trade, as the Act forbade the import of goods to Britain from Asia, Africa or America except by ships belonging to any of these countries or to Britain. As there were no Asiatic ships capable of the long voyage, it left the Company with the only ships engaged in the ever-increasing tea trade, much to the annoyance of other British traders who continually tried to break the monopoly, meanwhile indulging in smuggling with the use of foreign owned vessels.

However the lack of legal competition did not inspire the Honourable Company to improve the performance of their vessels, and voyages were tedious and hazardous, taking as much as eighteen months or more each way, carried out in a leisurely fashion with the ritual of lowering topgallant masts at night or whenever a squall threatened, and calls were made at intermediate ports for Company personnel or troops to be exchanged. They often carried a spare set of topgallant masts of shorter height which they interchanged according to the prevailing weather.

The precious tea cargo was frequently damaged and seldom fresh.

1 American *Rainbow*, 1845, built by Smith & Dimon, New York, and designed by J W Griffiths

Both black and green tea were shipped from China, the green being sent on to America where it was preferred. An extract from the logbook of the East Indiaman *Latham* on a two year homeward trip from Canton and Whampoa gives an insight into the perils to which the cargo was subject.

1785—May—Saturday the 28th—At St Helena. AM sent on shore the remainder of the St Helena stores. Found a box of Sugar Candy, Hon. Company's No. 51 had been washed out. Broke out and found several chests of Teas had been wet, it appearing that the Water in the Gale of Wind had been 18 in. high in the Gun Room on the starboard side.

The tea consisted of 1,000 chests of Congou and Bohea, and the damage had resulted from the starboard quarter gallery being washed away and the deadlights to the inner windows taking in the seas, and leaking badly for the remainder of the voyage.

The *Latham,* incidentally, while awaiting her cargo at Whampoa in December 1784, recorded the sailing thence of American ships *Empress of China,* Captain Green, and *Pallas,* Captain O'Donnel—the former vessel on her epoch-making voyage, being the first ship to carry the Stars and Stripes to China and carrying a letter from President Washington for the Chinese government officials.

Earlier in the 18th century, as the trade grew steadily, the British government had imposed a heavy tax on tea, against which the American colonists had protested, and although the tea tax was belatedly withdrawn for the colony, a heavy import duty was substituted with the all too well known consequence of the Boston Tea Party—and a temporary dislike for tea. The general tea tax in Britain was reduced in 1784, by which time America was instituting her own trade in prized oriental goods in exchange for furs, ginseng roots and silver, the latter chiefly in the nature of Mexican dollars which were the predominant form of exchange with the Chinese for centuries.

The Chinese government was originally reluctant to open up its ports to foreigners who, they claimed, could not offer anything of value to them which they did not already possess. They considered that they were bestowing a great favour in permitting trade at all—an opinion not shared by the local Hong merchants who were anxious to join in a profitable venture.

The port of Canton during the 18th century was the only one opened officially to the foreigners, who had to moor their ships in picturesque rows lower down the river at the Whampoa anchorage. They were allowed to establish 'factories' or warehouses for their resident representatives in a small colony stretching along the waterfront outside Canton. Each country had its elegant building of office and storehouse combined, set apart by fences and fronting onto private landing places, the whole scene enlivened by a row of tall flagpoles, each carrying a national flag, a scene often depicted in silk paintings and on porcelain bowls.

The relations between the Chinese merchants and their foreign counterparts were good, and frequent grand dinners and lavish entertainments were held in a great hall at Chinese expense. One merchant in particular, Houqua, earned a popular reputation with his integrity and courtesy and was a great favourite with all the merchants. One of the first clipper type American ships was named after him in 1844.

Despite the mutual understandings between the Chinese merchants and the foreigners, friction was constant with the government officials, occasioned for the most part by the persistent and iniquitous smuggling in of opium, the purchase of which was a drain on the Chinese silver, apart from its insidious effect on the population. Further irritation was caused by numerous small incidents with crew members on shore leave, and unfortunate deaths of local inhabitants resulting from the firing of the 'great guns' of passing ships in salute—a boisterous habit which also, at times, resulted in deaths of local inhabitants in British seaports.

The Honourable Company had difficulties in offering fair and acceptable exchange for their Chinese cargoes, especially with silver bullion, and therefore the easy availability of opium from their Indian possessions provided a profitable solution even though officially the Company had prohibited the sale of opium in 1796, at the same time as the Chinese government forbade its import. The need for fast small ships to escape detection by war junks or pirates, and capable of running into smaller ports along the coast to prohibited areas of Northern China, brought about a new breed of ships. By the 1830s both America and Britain were involved, and on a small scale some other European countries. America introduced fast smart schooners and brigs based on the lines of their Baltimore clippers, and the British equally successful schooners built by yards experienced with large seagoing yachts; one such famous craft, the schooner *Eamont*, having a main boom 110 ft long. Another British vessel, the *Falcon* of three-masted ship rig, had been built for Lord Yarborough as a yacht, and carried 22 guns. She was kept in perfect condition and manned with naval style discipline and efficiency like the East Indiamen.

By 1834 the East India Company had lost its monopoly of the China trade owing to the constant pressure from other groups of merchants, and the rapidly expanding trade brought on the urge to enter all the other Chinese ports along the coast. Attempts to do this had been made on a diplomatic level, Britain sending an ambassador, Lord Macartney, to Peking in 1792 with costly presents for the Emperor. The journey was

2 The triumphant arrival of the American *Oriental* in West India Dock, London, December 3, 1850

fruitless. Again in 1816 an attempt was made by Lord Amherst aboard a 46-gun naval frigate HMS *Alceste* accompanied by a naval brig, the *Lyra*, and an East Indiaman, the *General Hewitt*, which was also loaded with presents. Both of these expeditions failed by reason of what we would call in today's jargon a lack of communication, although both sides presented documents couched in the most distinguished language. The *Alceste* was wrecked on passage homewards off the coast of Sumatra and the Ambassador and his companions experienced many perils before reaching home.

Meanwhile the opium trade was irritating the Emperor and his officials such that they rigorously enforced their laws suddenly and inconveniently in 1839. The Emperor's Commissioner, Lin Tse Hsü, was a capable, intelligent man of high morals, respected by his British enemies. He was determined to eradicate the opium trade, confiscating and burning large quantities of opium; and in his eloquent letter to Queen Victoria he set forth the severest penalties for future offenders, with ample warnings, and requested Her Majesty's help in avoiding this necessity. Nevertheless a series of incidents resulted in war from 1840 to 1842, ending with the Treaty of Nanking, whereby Hong Kong was given to Britain and five Treaty Ports, Canton, Amoy, Foochow, Ningpo and Shanghai, were opened to Britain for free trade without the necessity of dealing through the officially licensed Hong merchants. Lin was banished in disgrace, although he was partially reinstated later, and had the unusual honour of having his effigy installed at Madame Tussaud's in London. New supplies of tea were now available to British traders, and two years later, the United States and France also contracted similar trading agreements.

In New York shipbuilders were making great strides in developing faster ships by departing from traditional theories, and their China trade was becoming increasingly profitable, the lighter cargoes enabling them to create finer lines. The *Rainbow* of 1845, built in New York (1), or possibly the *Houqua* of 1844, also from New York, may be said to have initiated the China clipper era.

Boston was not slow in following, the celebrated Donald McKay producing some of the finest clippers ever built. These vessels, apart from the lucrative China tea trade, were also showing their paces on the transatlantic passenger run, and from the East Coast of America round the Horn to San Francisco and across to Japan and China. The Gold Rush of 1848–9 also created an urgent demand for fast passages to California. The clippers on all of these routes were designed basically for passengers and light general cargoes, where speed of delivery was important. Prior to this era bulk cargoes as large in quantity as possible, with speed as a secondary consideration, were the chief desideratum.

Britain was also developing faster ships, but in isolated instances at first, until the Navigation Act was repealed in 1849, throwing British ports open to foreigners trading from the Far East.

The British-built clippers for the tea trade had an advantage over the American in that their designers knew what the intended cargo was and could estimate its weight and center of gravity beforehand, allowing for some slight variations in weights of different teas, and they could therefore design more precisely.

In the early 1840s Aberdeen had produced a new type of bow on small coastal schooners which had similarities to an American development and which, later in the decade, was being incorporated into tea trade ships, but it was the repeal of the Navigation Act which was instrumental in bringing much greater urgency to improving design. With the British ports now open to free competition, the Americans wasted no time in seizing their opportunity. Their clipper *Oriental*, built in New York in 1849, made her first voyage to Hong Kong and back to New York, the homeward leg taking 81 days. Her next trip back to Hong Kong took 80 days and some hours, which feat aroused the excited interest of British traders there, who immediately chartered her to take tea to London, where she arrived 97 days later, making a triumphant entry into the West India Dock on December 3, 1850 (2).

The whole nautical community was aroused with admiration for this magnificent fine-lined vessel, and no little uneasy at her threat to British ships. In drydock at Blackwall, the home of the East Indiamen and their successors the Blackwall frigates, surveyors and shipwrights took off her lines, a practice which had been carried out many times before with captured American or French ships noted for their speed and good sailing qualities, as later the lines of the yacht *America* and clipper *Challenge* were also taken off.

The only British sailing ship builders who had attracted any attention by experimenting with a new hull form and had achieved any noteworthy improvement were at this time located in Aberdeen, Messrs Hall and Messrs Hood, and it was to these builders that owners turned to meet the American threat.

The *Stornaway* and the *Chrysolite*, built by Halls in 1850 and 1851, were the immediate reply to the *Oriental*, the previous study of whose lines in London resulted in the Blackwaller *Challenger*, built by Greens of Blackwall in 1852.

The name *Challenger* was given to the British vessel as a reply to a much larger American clipper, the *Challenge*, a beautifully formed ship built in New York by Webb in 1851 (3). The *Challenger* was 174 ft long against the *Challenge's* length of 230 ft, and their first homeward passage together in 1852 has been the source of some argument, by those who tend to split up the true brotherhood of the sea along nationalistic lines like

3 Launch of the *Challenge* in 1851, Manhattan, New York

4 *Agamemnon* in Foochow, 1866

warring navies. The dates of departure and arrival were so close that a race is suggested, whereas other factors, involving the different departure ports, Whampoa and Shanghai, and the fact that the deep-drafted American had to wait three days in London for enough water to dock, rule this out. The American clipper *Nightingale* is also involved in the controversy, having left Shanghai three days after the *Challenger* and having conflicting dates, before and after, for arrival at Deal. During the following year, 1853, both the *Nightingale* and the *Challenger* left Woosung together, and the *Challenger* arrived two days ahead at Deal. Another American clipper, also called *Challenger,* was built in East Boston in 1853 and made a passage with tea in 1856 from China to London.

The American clippers in the 1850s outnumbered the handful of fast British clippers and took the best of the tea crop for some years, although individually some of them were well matched, the honours being about equal on both sides.

Unfortunately more incidents occurred with the Chinese authorities, and their seizure of a ship carrying the Union Jack under disputed circumstances brought on another war in 1856 during which Canton was blockaded and shelled, although some trade was still carried on with other ports, officials less patriotic than Lin being desirous of profits from opium. The treaty of Tientsin, concluded in 1858, opened up inland ports such as Hankow to the British and French and legalized the trade in opium on a limited scale. The East India Company was dissolved the same year, the pressure from other shipowners finally being effective.

A commercial treaty was also made with the United States, although by 1860 their clippers had withdrawn from the British trade, the *Flying Cloud* being the last ship to arrive in London with tea. Some of them continued carrying tea to New York for the next three years, and it is said that two old-timers, the barque *Maury* (later renamed *Benefactor*) and the *Golden State,* were able to pick up a tea cargo for New York each year until 1875. It is interesting to note that in 1858 two American clippers, the *Panama* and the *Picayune,* lying at Hong Kong and trading to the United States, were said to have had black crews, the former ship with the exception of the officers being entirely manned by them.

But for the majority of the American vessels hard driving had made their upkeep costly, and bad economic conditions at home, with an increasing lack of enthusiasm, forced their withdrawal. Their life was not over, however, and under reduced rig many of them did good work in other trades under the British and Dutch flags.

The race to bring fresh teas home was now between rival British owners, and the trade reached its peak with the composite clippers of the 1860s. Steamships up to this period had not constituted a real threat to sailing clippers on long voyages like the China run, owing to their need to refuel frequently at coaling stations off a direct route. As early as the 1830s small steam vessels owned by the EIC were sailing from India to Suez, chiefly with mails and passengers, and other steam vessels were operating in the Far East in localized voyages. In 1860 the screw steamship *Scotland* made the first visit to Hankow from Shanghai, followed in 1863 by the *Robert Lowe* which loaded a cargo direct from Hankow to London of 11,800 chests, half chests and boxes of tea together with cotton and sundry other items. This was the first intimation of a threat to the sailing clippers, and it became a reality by 1866 when an enterprising Liverpool shipowner, Alfred Holt, established the Ocean Steam Ship Company, known locally as the Blue Funnel Line. His first vessel, the *Agamemnon,* was unique in having the propeller aft of the rudder, but more important, she had a new type of economical engine with compound cylinders for high and low pressures. She also carried forty passengers in deckhouse cabins.

The *Agamemnon* made her first trip outwards via Mauritius, Penang, Hong Kong and Shanghai, returning by Foochow to pick up tea and then to the same ports homewards. One can imagine the emotions of those aboard the clippers as they lay in the Pagoda Anchorage, Foochow, when this sleek square-rigged steamship glided past (4). Her outward passage from Liverpool was made in 80 days to Shanghai, and homewards to London in 86 days, and the same year two sister vessels, the *Ajax* and *Achilles,* joined her, thus inaugurating a service of first rate ships to the Far East which has continued unbroken up to the present day, except for a period in World War II, the familiar tall blue funnel becoming almost a permanent seamark on the China Seas.

Steamships also had the advantage of their own derricks and steam-driven winches which rapidly increased the loading and discharging rates, especially in ports where they had to lie in an open roadstead. The opening of the Suez Canal in 1869, with its great reduction in distance together with additional coaling stations, brought into being a new race of steam clippers, and the sailing tea clippers had slowly vanished from the tea trade in racing form by the mid-1870s.

A few composite clippers were being built in 1869 and continued with the earlier ones to struggle for inferior tea cargoes, which they carried to the American shores, Australia, and at intervals to England, until about 1886, the *Halloween* being the last. Their life was not over, however, and with the addition of the new iron clipper the wool and emigrant trades to Australia and New Zealand still proved economical enough to keep them going, and on occasions to outpace their propeller driven rivals, even with rigs much reduced from those carried during the peak of the tea trade. One or two managed to earn a living into the next century, the *Cutty Sark* being an obvious example. Incidentally, during the reconstruction of the *Cutty Sark* in 1957, the master rigger for the restoration mentioned to me that as a boy he had sailed as late as 1924 in a smart little barque, rigged with main skysail yard and stuns'ls. This was the iron-hulled *E J Spence* built in Sunderland in 1871 and trading between Mauritius and Australia. Although not a tea clipper, she was probably the last vessel of that era to sail with such a rig on a purely commercial basis.

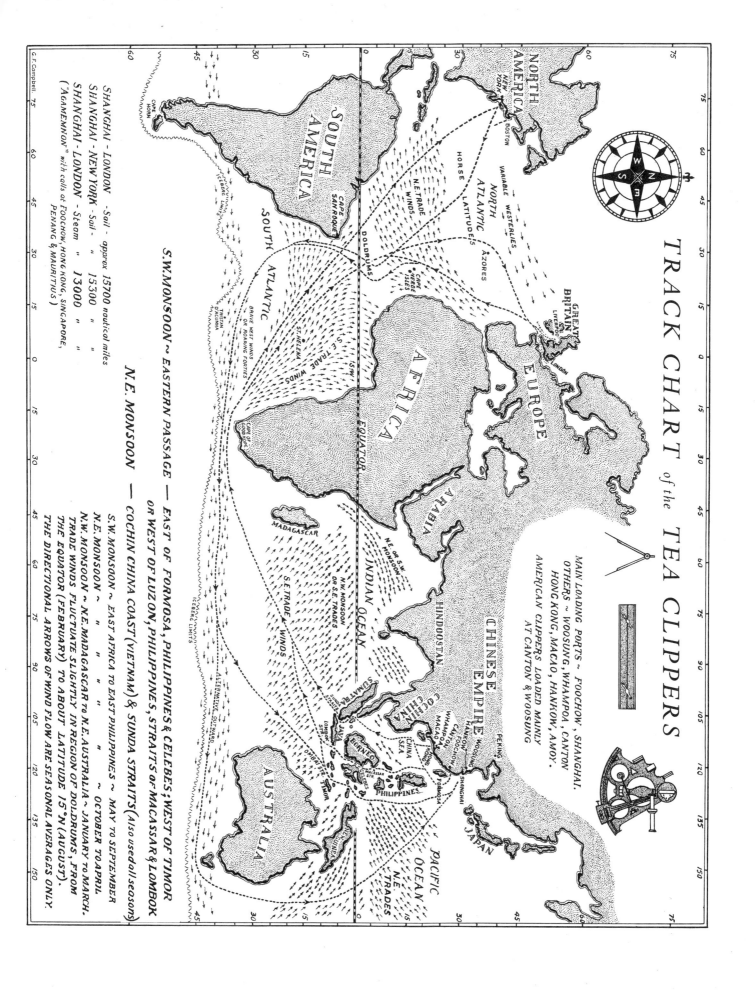

TRACK CHART of the TEA CLIPPERS

MAIN LOADING PORTS ~ FOOCHOW, SHANGHAI.
OTHERS ~ WOOSUNG, WHAMPOA, CANTON
HONG KONG, MACAO, HANKOW, AMOY.
AMERICAN CLIPPERS LOADED MAINLY
AT CANTON & WOOSUNG

**S.W. MONSOON ~ EASTERN PASSAGE — EAST OF FORMOSA, PHILIPPINES & CELEBES; WEST OF TIMOR
OR WEST OF LUZON, PHILIPPINES, STRAITS OF MACASSAR & LOMBOK**

N.E. MONSOON — COCHIN CHINA COAST (VIETNAM) & SUNDA STRAITS (Also used all seasons)

S.W. MONSOON ~ EAST AFRICA TO EAST PHILIPPINES ~ MAY TO SEPTEMBER
N.E. MONSOON ~ ~ OCTOBER TO APRIL.
N.W. MONSOON ~ N.E. MADAGASCAR to N.E. AUSTRALIA ~ JANUARY to MARCH.
TRADE WINDS FLUCTUATE SLIGHTLY IN REGION OF DOLDRUMS, FROM
THE EQUATOR (FEBRUARY) TO ABOUT LATITUDE 15°N (AUGUST).
THE DIRECTIONAL ARROWS OF WIND FLOW ARE SEASONAL AVERAGES ONLY.

SHANGHAI - LONDON   - Sail - approx 15700 nautical miles
SHANGHAI - NEW YORK - Sail - " 15300 "
SHANGHAI - LONDON   - Steam " 13000 "
("AGAMEMNON" with calls at FOOCHOW, HONG KONG, SINGAPORE,
PENANG & MAURITIUS)

G.F. Campbell

Chapter Two

The Homeward Passage

The time for loading tea depended much upon the seasonal crops, which were in two seasons for the export market and picked in April and June. The first crop brought high prices, and was loaded from about May or June. The favourite port for the earliest crop was Foochow, a port situated many miles inland up the Min River, which in parts is a narrow tortuous gorge. Other ports were Canton, Whampoa, Macao, Shanghai and later Hankow, where the clippers would load between June and August, with occasional sailings at other months of the year.

The most noteworthy races took place in the period between the late 1850s and the opening of the Suez Canal. After that time the clippers were searching for cargoes of inferior teas, usually from Shanghai, and sailing late in the year.

In 1859 there sailed from Foochow, within a few days of each other, *Fiery Cross, Ellen Rodger, Crest of the Wave, Ziba* and *Sea Serpent* (American), all arriving in London only a few days apart after approximately 140 days at sea. The American, having left last, arrived first in the Channel. Other close finishes were:

1861 *Ellen Rodger, Robin Hood, Falcon, Fiery Cross,* and *Flying Spur*

1866 *Ariel, Fiery Cross, Serica, Taeping, Falcon, Flying Spur, Black Prince, Chinaman, Ada, Coulnakyle* and *Taitsing*

1867 *Maitland, Serica, Taeping, Fiery Cross, Whiteadder, Zilba, Flying Spur, Taitsing, Black Prince, Yangtse, Ariel, Chinaman, Deerfoot, Min, Sir Lancelot, Belted Will* and *Eliza Shaw*

1869 *Ariel, Leander, Lahloo, Thermopylae, Spindrift, Taeping, Ziba, Sir Lancelot, Kaisow, Black Prince, Windhover, Serica, Falcon, Forward Ho, Titania, Taitsing, Whiteadder* and *Maitland*

1870 *Oberon, Titania, Cutty Sark, Serica, Forward Ho,* and *Belted Will*

1871 *Thermopylae, Forward Ho, Undine, Titania, Norman Court, Lahloo, Cutty Sark* and *Ariel*

The following list of typical passages, in days, from the different ports to England will give an idea of the fastest and slowest passages.

Canton to Liverpool   87, 99, 110, 130
Canton to London   99, 104, 115, 128, 134
Foochow to London   89, 93, 97, 144, 146
Shanghai to Liverpool   85, 87, 117, 122, 140
Shanghai to London   90, 92, 96, 100, 111, 129, 138, 166
Whampoa to Liverpool   88, 106, 126, 136, (*Scawfell,* 1861: 88 days)
Whampoa to London   92, 96, 112, 122, 128
Macao to London   89, 93, 96, 106, 117, 125

The famous *Cutty Sark* was not built until 1869 and consequently did not compete for long with other notable clippers, but made her reputation on the Australian run.

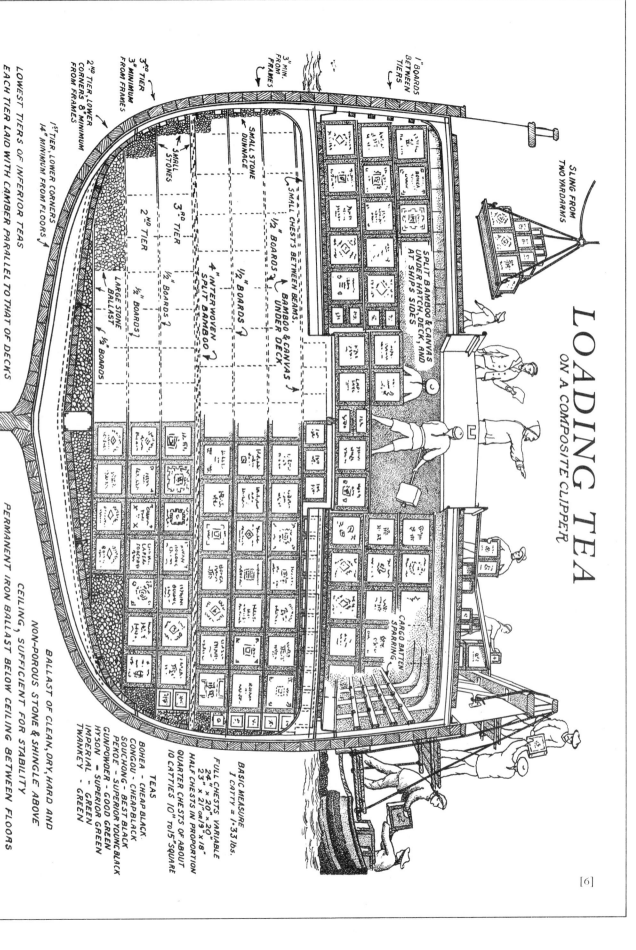

LOADING TEA
ON A COMPOSITE CLIPPER

SLING FROM TWO YARDARMS

1" BOARDS BETWEEN TIERS

3" MIN. FROM FRAMES

SMALL STONE DUNNAGE

SMALL STONES

SMALL CHESTS BETWEEN BEAMS.

BAMBOO & CANVAS UNDER DECK

½" BOARDS

½" BOARDS

½" BOARDS

½" BOARDS

INTERWOVEN SPLIT BAMBOO

3RD TIER

2ND TIER

LARGE STONE BALLAST

SPLIT BAMBOO & CANVAS UNDER HATCH, DECK AND AT SHIP'S SIDES

CARGO BATTEN SPARRING

3RD TIER 3" MINIMUM FROM FRAMES

2ND TIER, LOWER CORNERS 8" MINIMUM FROM FRAMES

1ST TIER, LOWER CORNERS 14" MINIMUM FROM FLOORS

LOWEST TIERS OF INFERIOR TEAS
EACH TIER LAID WITH CAMBER PARALLEL TO THAT OF DECK'S
STOWAGE COMMENCES AT SIDES & WORKS TOWARDS CENTRE

BALLAST OF CLEAN, DRY, HARD AND
NON-POROUS STONE & SHINGLE ABOVE
CEILING, SUFFICIENT FOR STABILITY
PERMANENT IRON BALLAST BELOW CEILING BETWEEN FLOORS
AVERAGE TOTAL BALLAST 350 TONS

BASIC MEASURE
1 CATTY = 1·33 lbs.

FULL CHESTS VARIABLE
24" × 20" × 20"
23" × 21" or 19" × 18"
HALF CHESTS IN PROPORTION
QUARTER CHESTS OF ABOUT
10 CATTIES 10" to 15" SQUARE

TEAS
BOHEA – CHEAP BLACK
CONGOU – CHEAP BLACK
SOUCHONG – BEST BLACK
PEKOE – SUPERIOR YOUNG BLACK
GUNPOWDER – GOOD GREEN
HYSON – SUPERIOR GREEN
IMPERIAL – GREEN
TWANKEY – GREEN

An instance of good straight racing between individual vessels occurred in 1866 with *Taeping* docking 20 minutes ahead of *Ariel,* the *Serica* being a few hours later on the same tide. The times were 99, 101 and 99 days respectively from Foochow.

The 1867 race was remarkable in that seven ships, *Whiteadder, Ziba, Taitsing, Black Prince, Yangtze, Chinaman* and *Deerfoot* arrived on the same day in London after 123, 121, 120, 119, 117 and 115 days from Foochow, with *Deerfoot* 125 days from Whampoa.

1868 saw *Ariel, Taeping* and *Sir Lancelot* leaving Foochow together, followed the next day by *Spindrift,* and arriving in London 97, 102, 98 and 97 days later.

In 1872 *Cutty Sark* and *Thermopylae* left Shanghai together, *Thermopylae* arriving in London seven days ahead, due only to the *Cutty Sark* having lost her rudder and having to finish with a jury one.

A great deal of controversy had been aroused in the past as to the actual speed of the clippers, and sailing ships in general. The methods used for computing speeds varied from a patent log to the old style log and glass, and it has been stated that the inaccuracies of the latter allowed exaggeration; but one could also logically say it may have underestimated speed as well.

Lord of the Isles was reputed to have reached 18 knots, *Spray of the Ocean* 17, and *Cutty Sark* $17\frac{1}{2}$ knots with a day's run of 363 miles. *Ariel* and *Thermopylae* did 16 knots, and 14 to 15 knots was quite usual with many clippers.

Speeds of 21 knots have been claimed and disputed by experienced mariners, in the correspondence columns of seaport newspapers at various times. Donald McKay specified his *Sovereign of the Seas* as being a 21 knot ship, so it must have been a reasonable figure for such an experienced designer to forecast it. In recent years I was informed by an officer of the USS *Eagle* that during a gale the ship had logged 21 knots measured by the most modern recording apparatus, and this was in a fairly full-lined vessel with a high deck structure and a feathered propeller. The sailmaker of the three-masted steel ship *Brenda* of 1891, a full-bodied cargo carrier, used to tell me that on a number of occasions she logged 19 knots.

Captain Clark, in his book *The Clipper Ship Era,* records the American *Lightning* and the *James Baines* Blackball liner on the Liverpool–New York run logging speeds of $18\frac{1}{2}$ and 17 to 21 knots. These Donald McKay creations, together with his other noble ships, were probably the finest and fastest sailing vessels ever built. The whole value of the clipper ships, however, lay not only in their ability to attain high speeds under ideal conditions for short periods, but in being able to move at all when most other vessels were becalmed, and in maintaining good average speeds for all conditions. A great deal depended on the commander, the great variety of hull forms giving only individual advantage under certain conditions. It is fair therefore to say that 10 to 12 knots was a good all-round speed.

There has never been an event so grand in its scope as a race between tea clippers from China to England, requiring as it did the fullest measure of human endurance, skill, courage and expert knowledge. The races were not organized events with an even start on the firing line—the prime motive behind them was strictly business. But as the tea industry was a seasonal affair, groups of vessels would congregate together to load up from their various sources of supply. Sometimes a vessel would be loaded, all her official papers completed and a tug taking her to the open sea, when the master of another ship, seeing this, would hastily finish loading and without waiting for the completion of official formalities would get his ship moving in a frantic endeavour to catch up with his rival.

From this moment followed the long passage home through gales, calm belts, fair winds and foul—the ships sighting each other only to lose contact again. Sometimes one ahead, sometimes the other, each displaying her better qualities under the varying conditions. One ship would ghost along under a whisper of a breeze, to the chagrin of the other lying as motionless as a derelict in a backwater. In heavy weather the positions might reverse; the latter ship romping along with effervescent foam sizzling past her waist, and nature's energy pulling with a hundred fingers from the corners of every available stitch of canvas—even odd scraps of tarpaulin, boat covers and blankets might be harnessed to the cause. In contrast her companion would gradually drop astern over the horizon, her sail reduced for fear of driving the ship beyond her ability. Then other ships from different loading ports would join in the race as the routes to home waters converged on the main track.

The route from China was perilous enough from the moment a ship left her anchorage, quite apart from the monsoons. The Min River from the Pagoda Anchorage at Foochow was a narrow gorge with a fast-flowing current (10). Old-timers used to say that the opposite banks were so close that monkeys jumping across got their tails entangled in the brace blocks. Several clippers met their fate entering or leaving this passage, as, if either the heel or forefoot touched the bank they would be swung round by the current, heel over losing stability, and lie half submerged at an angle in a matter of minutes. They would then be stripped of all movable parts by local fishermen or pirates as quickly as the wreckers or looters on the wild coast of Britain in the old days would clean out a hull. This was the fate of the *Oriental* in 1853 and the British *Vision* in 1857, to name but two of many.

7 *Titania* overhauling *Thermopylae*, 1871

8 *Thermopylae* shortening sail before a squall

9 Waiting for tea at the Pagoda Anchorage, Foochow

Mention of looters recalls an amusing incident entirely unconnected with the China trade, when Sir Walter Scott was on a tour of Scottish lighthouses in 1814, and commented on the poor condition of the sails of a crofter's boat. The crofter replied, 'If it had been His will that you hadna built sae many lighthouses hereabouts, I wad have had new sails last winter.'

The route from Northern China was either east of Formosa, the Philippines and Celebes, then through the Ombai Straits west of Timor; or else east of Formosa, west of the Philippines, through the Macassar Straits between Borneo and Celebes, and into the Indian Ocean by the Lombok Straits. This route would be used during the SW monsoons between May and September.

The more usual route from the southern ports and occasionally the northern was down through the China Sea, off the Cochin China coast, known today as the tragic Viet Nam, then between Sumatra and Java through the old passage of the Sunda Straits and past the well known Anjer Point where native craft would crowd around offering their wares.

The China Sea in those days was badly charted and the numerous shoals and reefs still bear the names of clippers which were abruptly halted in their eager flight as they tore their hulls open on the jagged barriers; if lucky, to pass over minus a false keel and much copper; if not, to lie there stripped by pirates, slowly disintegrating in the tropical sun. Names like Rifleman Bank, Fiery Cross and Lizzie Weber Reef, and Scawfell Shoal immortalize names which might have otherwise ended ignominiously nailed to the side of a shipbreaker's hut.

More southerly, off the Isle of Bangka in the Java Sea, where the ill-fated *Alceste* with Lord Amherst aboard came to grief in 1816, the same reef sealed the fate of other clippers such as the British *Lammermuir* and the American *Memnon*, which was one of the pioneer group, built in New York in 1848.

Compared with other vessels (both naval and merchant) sailing the seas in those days, there is no doubt that the masters of the tea clippers took many risks in their desire for speed. It is said that they were remarkably young, because older and wiser men had the experience and imagination to know when to take safety measures. However that is not to say that the clipper masters were all of a foolhardy type. The best of them took risks with a full awareness of the consequences.

Tales are told of masters who would put padlocks on the sheets before retiring below, thus preventing any reduction in the sail area by the watchkeeping mate. Yet while such tales may be regarded only as impressive yarns for the foc's'le, they do indicate the general eagerness to keep moving fast at almost all costs. Sometimes, however, a good ship with excellent sailing qualities would be restrained by an over-cautious master, and a more confident man would take a delight in rubbing it in, by literally sailing in circles round him. He would overhaul the cautious one and, when some distance ahead, deliberately hold back until he had dropped astern on the other side, and then spurt ahead again hailing his fellow with choice and sarcastic language.

It was remarkable how the ships so often kept pace with one another over a distance of some 15,700 miles. Leaving China together they might not see one another for ninety days or so until, nearing the English Channel in the first light of dawn, they would perhaps find themselves again in company.

The approach to the entrance to the Channel was another hazard which many ships failed to overcome. From the Bay of Biscay the tea clippers' route was either northwards to Liverpool or eastwards for London. To quote from a Channel pilot's guidebook of the 1830s *The New Seaman's Guide and Coaster's Companion*,

> Ships coming into the Channel ought always if possible to make the land about the Lizard: for should they afterwards have thick weather, they will know how to steer and how advance up the Channel—when coming from the southward into the Channel in thick weather and light winds, they frequently get much to the northward of account, and fall into the Bristol Channel. In running up the course from the Lizard to the Start go not into less water than 40 fathoms, for 35 fathoms are in the stream of the Eddystone and you will by keeping without that depth go quite clear of that danger. By being too far to the southward and mistaking the Casket Lights at first sight for those of Portland, has often proved fatal and occasioned the loss of many ships upon the dangers adjacent.

However if the wind was favourable and the weather clear, the last leg up the Channel was often an exciting finale calling for the utmost endeavour and seamanship. Tugboats would be ignored as long as possible, and maybe a clipper could pass the Goodwins, round the headland at Margate and be well past the ancient Reculvers marks up the Thames estuary before taking a tow. Towards either destination, as soon as a ship was sighted at a semaphore signal station a message would be relayed from hilltop to hilltop in a matter of a few seconds to the owners in either London or Liverpool. Heading for Liverpool the first sighting would be made at Holyhead and by means of a semaphore telegraph consisting of six movable arms on a pole, which could transmit a number code, a message could be sent to Liverpool 72 miles away in about 15 seconds, the record being 9 seconds. This was by way of nine intermediate stations, the last one being on a hill overlooking the town, where a series of flagpoles would each fly an owner's flag as soon as their vessel entered the river. A

10 *Norman Court* navigating the Min River and drifting with a kedge

11 Tropical evenings

12 *Fiery Cross*, 1860

13 *Lahloo* drives a hard bargain

similar semaphore system operated from the South Coast near Portland, to London. The shipowners also had weathervanes erected above their offices which were geared to compass clocks, one inside the boardroom and one facing the street, which gave them some indication of the prevailing wind and whether their investment would dock in good time. Some of these old clocks were in existence up to recent days, and the old telegraphs are remembered by the many localities still retaining the name 'Telegraph Hill'.

It was natural for the hardheaded masters to avoid the towline as long as practicable, but they sometimes regretted it. One can picture a paddle tug wallowing within hailing distance, its black sulphureous smoke threatening to befoul the white splendour of the clipper's sails, and an irate mate threatening to pour a bucketful of water down the tug's funnel to put the fire out. One clipper, having made the Channel ahead of a rival, was making such good time that her master refused the help of the best tug, which thereupon disappeared astern and picked up the rival. The wind easing off later, the rival under tow soon overhauled the first ship, which by this time was able only to secure the services of a much less powerful tug and lost the race to the final docking in consequence. Each tug had a fixed rate depending on the distance and its horsepower, varying between 40 and 100, so it was a temptation to hold on as long as possible before hiring a less powerful tug for the short end of the voyage. But the bargaining and banter would reach its inevitable end with a handshake via the towrope, when the clipper would deflate her filling sails, snug down and meekly submit to being led into the dock to her well earned rest.

In contrast with the somewhat anticlimactic end of voyage in London, some sixty-odd miles up the Thames, clippers arriving in Liverpool could make quite a thrilling finish. With favourable winds, after picking up the pilot off the Welsh coast and ignoring the aid of a tug, they would carry on under full sail through the channelways of the estuary and up the River Mersey for about three miles until opposite the port, where they would furl sail and drop anchor in the crowded waterway with the precision and speed of a well trained naval ship. American ships in particular were wont to do this, to the enthusiastic cheers of onlookers.

Chapter Three

Development of the Ships

The form and rig of ocean-going, cargo carrying merchant ships through-out earlier centuries had been primarily adopted for the carriage of as much cargo as possible. The slow, lumbering argosies of Spain were in keeping with the general pace of life in their day, which changed little until the 19th century. The complete dependence on wind power with the absence of power-driven tugboats often meant a delay in leaving an estuary of days, weeks, and sometimes months. Whole fleets of a hundred or more East Indiamen and varied craft could be seen in the bay off the Isle of Sheppey at the mouth of the Thames, for days on end, as also in the Downs awaiting a fair wind. One instance is recorded of two ships leaving Liverpool on the same day, one of which caught a wind which took her to the West Indies. Upon her return to Liverpool she found the other ship still waiting for enough wind to move her. In contrast to this, another eyewitness in 1828 gives a delightful description of 140 ships sailing out of the river on one tide, with their sails stretching as far as the eye could see down the channel.

The system of assessing a ship's size in the 18th century, for taxation or harbour dues and for its own valuation in building cost or sale or charter, was based on the assumption that the physical proportions of length, beam, depth and hull shape between light and load line were approxi-mately the same for all ships, which was a reasonable assumption for the time. The value of a ship was considered to lie in the weight of cargo it would carry, and therefore a formula was evolved whereby the actual volume of a ship's hull between the light and load drafts (the deadweight capacity) could be easily assessed and converted into equivalent weight in tons of seawater. It should be remembered that many vessels were built more or less by rule of thumb with the minimum, if any, of builders' drawings on which to make calculations. This assessment of deadweight or burden (burthen) was in tons of weight, known as Builder's Tonnage, and in use officially up to 1836, after which it was referred to as Builder's Old Measure.

The formula used the length of keel, the beam, and for the depth be-tween light and load line, a proportion of the beam, the product of these three figures being divided by a factor which gave actual tons weight. In the event of the ship having no certificate originally, the Customs officer could measure the assumed length of keel with the vessel afloat, by means of a formula which made appropriate deductions from a length measured between certain perpendiculars above the waterline. Un-fortunately there were loopholes in this assessment, of which unscrupulous shipowners took advantage. Within the confines of the standard shape of block which these measurements gave, a ship could be either very bulky or slim, yet giving the same resultant tonnage, because the actual depth to the keel could be increased dangerously without increasing the tonnage figure, which had originally been intended for vessels of a reasonable depth. Undue depth of hull was used all too often, resulting in an unseaworthy and inefficient ship which, however, satisfied greed and allowed the extra stowage height for West Indian sugar or whatever cargo the owners dealt in. To make matters still worse, there was at that time no regulation which fixed the maximum draft to which a vessel could be loaded to ensure a safe height of freeboard.

The stories that have been written about the 'coffin ships' in the 19th century are not exaggerated, and on many occasions a crew was sent to its doom by the force of law, after having unwittingly signed on a crank and grossly overloaded ship. In 1840 an average of $1\frac{1}{2}$ ships per day of those in Lloyd's Register were lost, from all causes. The assessment of a safe load line was left to the discretion of the owner, and freeboard used to be 'guessed' at about one-eighth of the beam.

By 1835 Lloyd's had proposed a freeboard of 3 in. per foot depth of hold, which was not compulsory, however; and it was not until 1854 that draft marks at stem and stern were made compulsory by Act of Parliament, although many ships carried them for their own convenience long before this time. In the golden days of Venice, merchants had a maximum draft mark made in the shape of a leaden diamond or cross nailed on the side of their galleons, which showed a healthy concern for the safety of their ships. In Britain many efforts were made to make ships safer and in 1876 the first fixed load line marking, a diamond with a horizontal line each side of it, and the letters LR, was required by Lloyd's for a certain class of vessel only, known as 'awning decked' and built with light superstructures. Even this measure was opposed by one prominent shipowner, who fortunately lost a lawsuit when trying a test action against it. It was at this time that the well known figure of Mr Samuel Plimsoll MP was prominent in Parliament, fighting for the greater safety of ships, and in the same year, 1876, through his efforts an Act of Parliament was passed whereby all vessels had to carry a load line marking of a circle with a horizontal line through its center—the familiar Plimsoll line. This mark did not necessarily have the letters LR on it, but letters, if any, appropriate to the society under which it was classified, which could be foreign. This Plimsoll line, however, was not fixed in a definite position by any mathematical computation, but was decided at the owner's discretion for any particular cargo he intended, the amount of freeboard being arbitrary. Lloyd's experts meanwhile were preparing tables of freeboard assessed in a more scientific way and were encouraged in this endeavour by the majority of shipowners, who asked for guidance with their load line markings, and by 1886 tables were supplied and the non-obligatory mark of the circle and horizontal line was used for a fixed position. It was not made compulsory for all vessels until the Merchant Shipping Act of 1890. It should be noted that Lloyd's load line mark for ships registered with them was not the same thing as a Government mark.

Reverting back to the question of tonnage under the Old Measure, although some owners took dangerous advantage of its loopholes, reputable owners such as the East India Company took advantage only to the extent of producing good heavy cargo carriers with little pretension to speed, but which were considered safe.

One restraining factor in British design of merchant ships for the period covering the latter part of the 18th and the early 19th centuries resulted from the almost continuous state of war, which necessitated ships travelling in convoys whose speed was regulated by the slowest vessel. The convoys, which could take a couple of months in assembling, were made compulsory by an Act of 1798, although there were special exemptions if a ship was considered fast enough and sufficiently well armed.

American and other Northern European ships by contrast sailed singly, and consequently studied new forms and gained more practical knowledge. An American ship was estimated to make a passage in about two-thirds of the time of a British ship, although it sacrificed capacity in order to do so. The continental European builders applied more scientific knowledge to their ships, since their men of science, especially in France and Sweden, applied themselves to the theoretical knowledge of naval architecture. British theory was sadly lacking in the first thirty years or so of the 19th century, an attempt at forming a school of study having failed owing to opposition from the old school of naval constructors, although the practical aspect of ship construction advanced and workmanship itself was of the highest class in the best shipyards and dockyards.

The need for speed did exist, however, in other uses of ships, and fine-lined fast vessels had been operating for some centuries before, notably the privateers, smugglers, dispatch vessels, naval cutters and coastal packets. Smaller craft such as skiffs, wherries, fishing smacks and yachts had fine lines chiefly as a result of a natural form arising from their mode of construction with light planking. Hollow lines were also known from ages back, but there was an unwritten law that hollow lines must be filled in for the larger ocean-going ships, aided no doubt by the desire for as much cargo capacity as possible. The development of the steam vessel in the early part of the 19th century cannot be overlooked in considering the advent of the clipper type. A good example of early steamship lines can still be seen in Lucerne, Switzerland, where the lake paddle boat *Rigi*, a 138 ft iron-hulled vessel built in 1847 by Ditchburn & Mare, London, is preserved. Her bow lines can truly be described as knife-like, with hollow waterlines and hollow sections. There seems to have been more freedom of thought applied to steamship design, possibly because their lines could be considered from the fact that their normal position was upright, both sides of the ship being symmetrical, whereas with a sailing vessel, although the lines are symmetrical when upright, they become asymmetrical with the vessel in its usual position heeled over to one side. Wherein lies the true skill in forming good lines for a sailing ship, as the amount of heel has to be assessed, from the sail area and the position of its centre of effort, under the weather conditions most likely to be met on a given route, together with the stability necessary for this, which in turn depends also on the nature of the cargo carried as well as the lines.

Scott Russell, an eminent naval architect of the mid-19th century, and one of a very small number who could apply scientific principles to design, used to assert that the most important part of a sailing vessel's lines were the shoulders, those parts of the vessel's hull which were immersed or emerged when heeled, and which provided the resistance to too much heeling. This area had to be well formed so that it did not produce un-balanced resistance at either end. The lateral profile of the ship, length and draft, had also to be considered from its effect in providing resistance to making leeway. The above-water hull itself could act as a long un-adjustable sail offering resistance which could vary according to the amount of concave flare in the bows, and its height, a feature which was lessened in some of the low-profile Aberdeen clippers, which also stowed their boats on deck thereby reducing the windage still more. A sharp and square forefoot with a deep keel would help to keep a vessel on course but would also offer resistance to changing course quickly. A vessel with a flat bottom or nearly so, and a small round bilge, could be heeled over such that the bilge became more immersed than the keel, and if the fullest area of the bilge was too far forward or aft, would throw the hull out of balance, requiring careful adjustment of the balance of sail. A good rise of floor could also become a flat bottom when heeled over too much.

All of these points had to be considered by the designer and the best compromise arrived at since they could not all be satisfied equally. The question of the upward lateral slope of the bottom known as the rise of floor was one which concerned the early designers very much, some considering a pronounced slope best for speed. Shipowners were at first opposed to this as it meant a loss of internal capacity also.

Designers did not usually have an entirely free hand with their designs but were subject to the owners' wishes, and the owners were frequently retired shipmasters themselves with pronounced ideas on how their ships were to be built. Webb, the versatile and ingenious New York ship-builder, commented on one of his draughts that the ship had too much rise of floor, at the owners' request, and was not as good a sailer as his own judgement would have made her.

On the other hand, with a vessel specifically designed for the tea trade where the stowage of square chests to the deck level required a flat level base on which to build upwards, the permanent iron ballast necessary could be conveniently stowed in the triangular space resulting from a good rise of floor, levelled off with the additional shingle ballast, this space being of little value for squared tier stowage.

Although the old tonnage law gave an advantage to the owner of the most unseaworthy type of ship, it did not prevent anyone designing a ship exactly as he wanted. It has often been stated that the law inhibited good design. This was true to the extent that many shipowners abused it and strenuously opposed any revision. Despite the fact that finer lines with less draft would result in a ship having to pay more tonnage dues proportionate to actual capacity than the badly designed ship, some ships were being built on improved lines ignoring the apparently inequitable taxation which resulted. This was particularly true in America, where as new ideas occurred they were tried out regardless. Also with steamships, the increased speed and profit apparently offered enough inducement to ignore the tonnage dues. In the coastal home trade with smaller vessels the tonnage dues were considerably below those of foreign-going vessels, and in consequence the former seem to have been ahead in their development, ignoring the fat little collier brig types where maximum capacity was desired, speed being of little consequence.

Actually the tonnage dues, etc. paid by a ship entering harbour were not as heavy as those who operated crank unsafe ships with untaxable excess cargo space, suggested. A ship entering a port had to pay, in the first instance, for the pilot, then possibly for a tugboat, and once in port, the local dock dues and light dues, the latter being for the maintenance of lighthouses, lightships, buoys etc. There might also be drydock or graving dock rates. The actual cargo carried was taxed on its manifest, item by item, down to the last button, from an extraordinarily comprehensive scale of charges, regardless of the ship's nominal tonnage.

Of these items, pilotage rates were based on the ship's draft at so much per foot, so that the deep-draft ship was actually at a disadvantage. This was a source of much dissatisfaction among the pilots, who complained that many foreign ships were increasing in length and tonnage but not draft and were still paying the old rates. They tried unsuccessfully to have the rates changed from footage to tonnage in 1854 and 1861. Tugboat rates were based on the distance towed and the power of the tug, which could be anything between 40 and 100 h.p. in the early days. Here again tonnage had no effect other than physical size affecting the choice of tug. Light dues and dock dues were based on the ship's tonnage.

Some typical charges for the year 1835 in the port of Liverpool were as follows:

Pilotage British vessels, outward, 4 shillings per foot; inward 4 shillings per foot and up to 9 shillings for maximum distance.

Towage 100 h.p. tug from Dock to NW Lightship, 14 guineas. 40 h.p. tug from Dock to NW Lightship: 8 guineas. Inward charges slightly less.

Light dues Vessels from overseas 1 penny per ton of register admeasurement.

Dock dues Varying for distance from overseas. Maximum from Pacific, 3 shillings per ton. Minimum home trade, 3 pence per ton.

Dry dock dues Two tides: 100 tons, £2.8.0.; 200 tons, £3.0.0.; 300 tons, £3.12.0.

It will be seen from these figures that the savings in tonnage dues from having an overloaded and unsafe ship were hardly worthwhile, but it was the old tale of getting something for nothing, and the growing practice of marine insurance did not help.

But many progressive minds were striving to get the tonnage law changed in the interests of humanity towards the seamen and commonsense progress in the ships. They were vigorously opposed and called schemers, agitators and revolutionists, this being a time of much social unrest, but eventually they were able to bring about a change by 1836, whereby the internal cubic capacity of the ship was calculated on a reasonable mathematical basis using internal cross-sectional areas, amidships and at one-sixth the length from each end of deck; which areas by a simple formula including the length and depth were converted into tons of capacity at 92·4 cu. ft per ton. This system of measurement was referred to as the New Measurement and was in use until 1854 when a much more accurate assessment of a ship's actual internal volume was initiated which gave tonnage capacity on the basis of 100 cu. ft per ton, which is still the basis today. A disadvantage or rather an inconvenience of both of the latter systems of tonnage measurement lay in the fact that measurements had to be made over certain members of the ship's internal structure. This meant that accurate detailed structural drawings had to be made before the ship was built in order to arrive at a specific tonnage. This was beyond the capability of quite a good number of otherwise competent builders, and for this reason they continued to quote prices for new vessels on the old measure (Builder's Measure), as also did shipowners when selling or chartering. Such vessels would have their official taxable tonnage assessed by whatever authority ruled in their first port of loading.

Although this new freedom, in killing the old excuse for a bulky ship, was said to have been the major impetus in improved design, the advantage gained for foreign-going British ships only applied to the homeward end of the voyage. America did not revise her old rules, which were

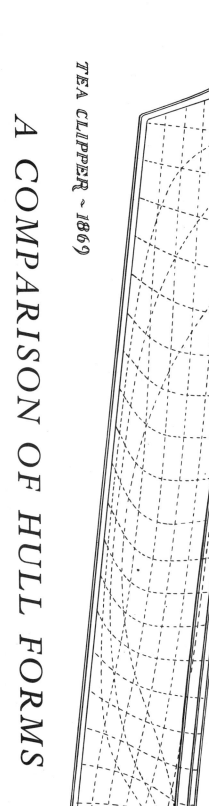

A COMPARISON OF HULL FORMS

TEA CLIPPER ~ 1869

EAST INDIAMAN ~ circa 1820

[14]

similar to the British Old Measurement, until 1865, and other nations at varying dates and later still, up to 1875. The real impetus to improving design in Britain therefore was competition.

The word 'clipper', of disputed origin, generally refers to a vessel with fine lines designed for speed at the expense of cargo capacity in the period when the average merchant ship had full lines. The earliest forms were small vessels, usually not foreign going except for the opium clippers. Their original growth of any consequence was on the East Coast of America, Baltimore claiming the initiative in 1833 with an enlarged version of an older schooner type, a ship called the *Ann McKim*, which had limited cargo capacity.

The packet ships on the New York–England run by this time were keeping to a regular ferry schedule and the demand for speed and increased size was becoming insistent. However it was not possible simply to take the old apple bowed full-bodied hulls and fine them down without some structural changes also.

To provide a good sail area in earlier times it was necessary to give a wide space between the fore and main mast so that sails on the latter did not blanket those on the foremast when braced around. The foremast was therefore kept well up near the bows and usually raked forward as well, to increase the distance still more. The hulls were proportionately shorter for the sail area compared with the late 19th century craft. In addition to the heavy weight of the foremast and all its gear up in the bows, the head of the ship itself was structured with ponderous overhanging knees to form a low-hung stem with elaborate timbers, trail boards, figurehead, anchors, catheads, bumpkins, spritsail spars, etc. all of which weight had to be supported by sufficient buoyancy in the underwater body of the bow. All ships also have to endure the situation of the forward part being suspended intermittently over the trough of a wave. The resultant strain of the downward bending moment eventually distorts the hull permanently out of shape in a condition known as hogged. The weight of the mainmast amidships also resulted frequently, in wooden ships, in a localized sag, so that a ship eventually could have an undulating sheer combining both hogging and sagging, the high over-burdened poops having the same effect as the heavy bow.

One of the first moves in lessening these consequences was to place the foremast further aft, which could be done with an increased length of hull, and then to reduce the size and weight of the structure of the upper stemhead work. The evolution came in stages. A reference to the drawing of the East Indiaman and tea clipper (14) will show the old style of heavy bow, and the drawing of the development of the clipper bow (15) gives the most significant steps in the change to the clipper type. New York was

DEVELOPMENT *of the* CLIPPER BOW

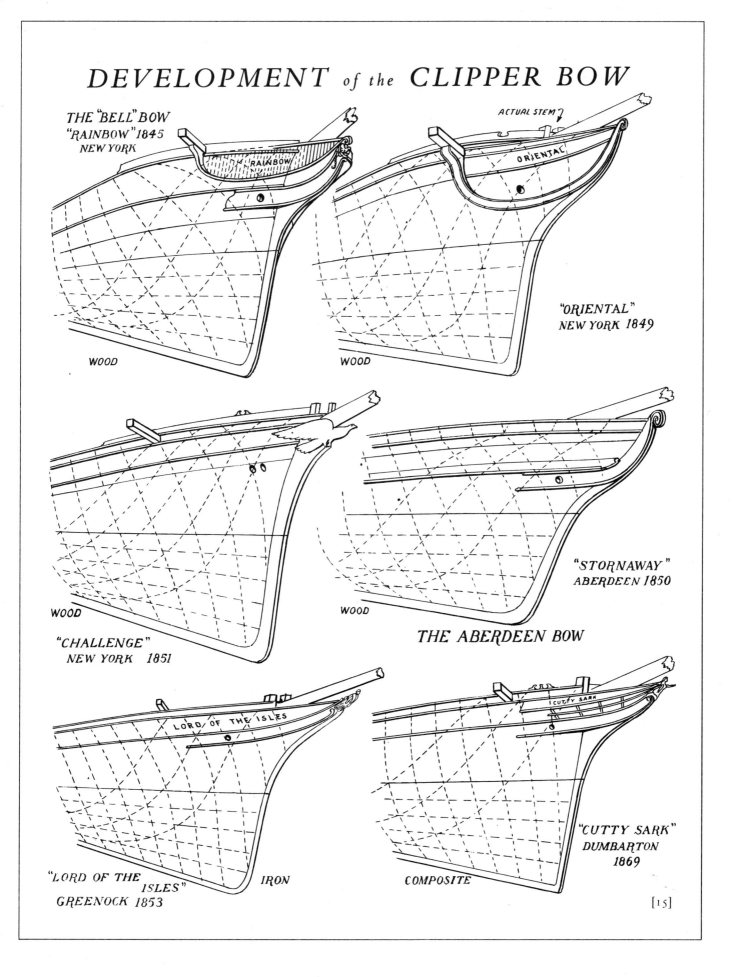

THE "BELL" BOW
"RAINBOW" 1845
NEW YORK

RAINBOW

WOOD

ACTUAL STEM

ORIENTAL

"ORIENTAL"
NEW YORK 1849

WOOD

"CHALLENGE"
NEW YORK 1851

WOOD

"STORNAWAY"
ABERDEEN 1850

WOOD

THE ABERDEEN BOW

LORD OF THE ISLES

"LORD OF THE
ISLES"
GREENOCK 1853

IRON

CUTTY SARK

"CUTTY SARK"
DUMBARTON
1869

COMPOSITE

the main centre for the change, the firms Brown & Bell, Smith & Dimon, and Webb & Allen setting the pace. On the transatlantic packets in the 1830s the bow had been refined below the waterline somewhat, but above this level it swelled out with a great flare and a full wide forecastle deck; the shape resembled an inverted bell and still had the rather heavy headboards and full, overhanging stemhead knees. Bell produced the *Houqua* in 1844 with this type of bow, for the China trade, and at the time it was considered to be a sharp ship initiating a new trend. The following year Smith & Dimon brought out the *Rainbow* which was finer still below the waterline, and the deck line was also less rounded and full. She has been called the first real clipper ship, a claim difficult to decide as this evolution was a gradual one involving change step by step above waterline and below. The finer underwater shape enabled a ship to be driven faster up to a certain sea condition, after which the overhanging upper part would hit the sea with a shock which momentarily tended to stop the ship's forward motion and severely strain the structure. The overhang or flare was considered necessary to provide buoyancy and prevent the ship's head nosing into or under a sea and also keep the decks relatively free from large masses of water. This it did up to a point, for in the old East Indiamen a veritable farmyard of livestock was able to survive on the upper deck since the ships were not driven hard in bad weather.

A talented young designer, John Griffiths, employed by Smith & Dimon in New York, had advocated a lengthened bow without the old-style encumbrances as early as 1841 and had designed the *Rainbow* of 1845, but it was not until 1847 when Brown & Bell built the *Samuel Russell* that it actually came about, followed in 1849 by the famous *Oriental*.

The chief characteristic of this type of bow was that the hull planking was carried forward beyond the original nearly upright stem and on to the extended stem knees, taking the place of the headboards. The drawings of the headworks and upper stem (17) show this change, where the drooping roundness of the overhang is also diminished and approaches more to the true clipper stem of the iron-hulled British clippers of later date.

This type of stem had additional buoyancy, and being neater, without exposed timbers, it cut into the rising seas without a retarding shock or flurry of water. The simplicity of this style was next carried further by diminishing the curving overhang until the termination of the hull planking (the 'hood' or 'wood' ends) was on a slightly curved line raking a little forward and the profile of the stem piece itself slightly more curved, finishing with a light unobtrusive knee which supported the figurehead and took the bowsprit gammoning. This arrangement reached its ultimate purity of form with the magnificent clipper ship *Challenge* launched in

THE WAY OF A SHIP

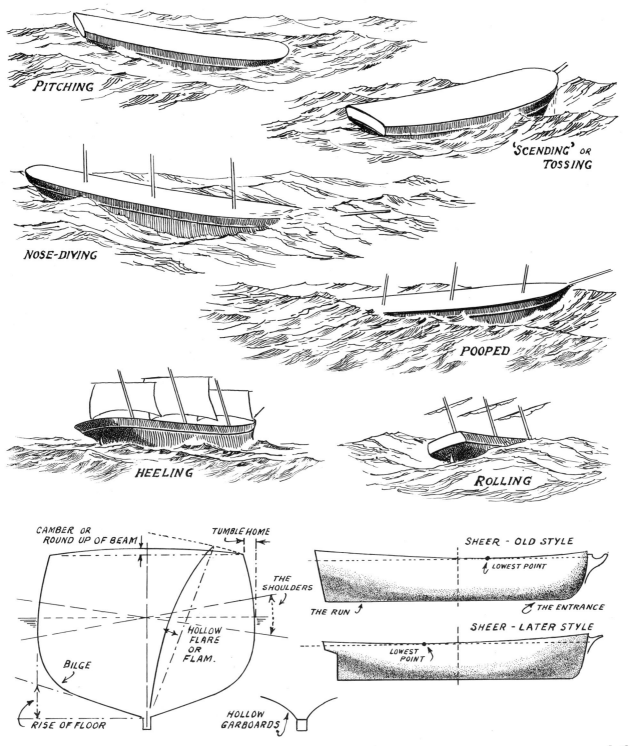

PITCHING

'SCENDING' OR TOSSING

NOSE-DIVING

POOPED

HEELING

ROLLING

CAMBER OR ROUND UP OF BEAM

TUMBLE HOME

THE SHOULDERS

HOLLOW FLARE OR FLAM.

BILGE

RISE OF FLOOR

HOLLOW GARBOARDS

SHEER – OLD STYLE

LOWEST POINT

THE RUN

THE ENTRANCE

SHEER – LATER STYLE

LOWEST POINT

[16]

HEADWORKS and UPPER STEM

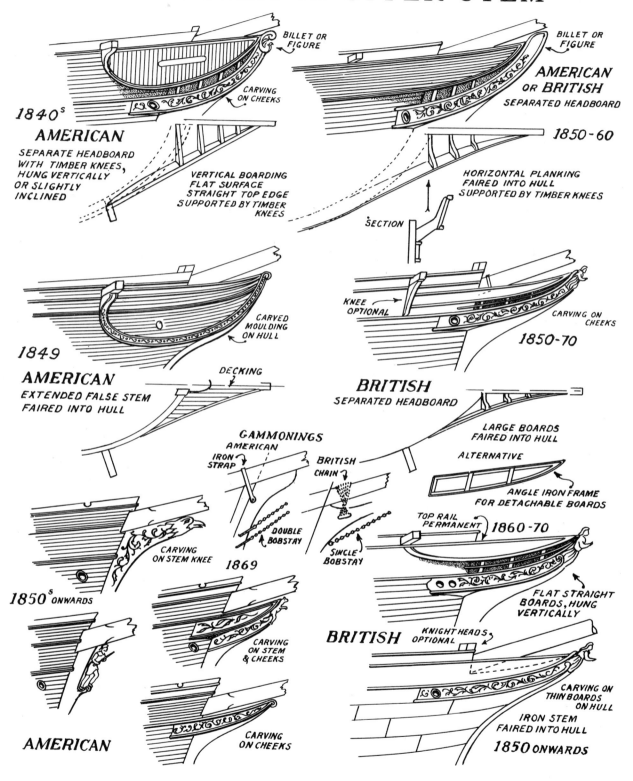

BILLET OR FIGURE

CARVING ON CHEEKS

1840ˢ
AMERICAN
SEPARATE HEADBOARD WITH TIMBER KNEES, HUNG VERTICALLY OR SLIGHTLY INCLINED

VERTICAL BOARDING FLAT SURFACE STRAIGHT TOP EDGE SUPPORTED BY TIMBER KNEES

BILLET OR FIGURE

AMERICAN OR BRITISH
SEPARATED HEADBOARD
1850-60

HORIZONTAL PLANKING FAIRED INTO HULL SUPPORTED BY TIMBER KNEES

SECTION

KNEE OPTIONAL

CARVING ON CHEEKS

1850-70

1849
AMERICAN
EXTENDED FALSE STEM FAIRED INTO HULL

CARVED MOULDING ON HULL

DECKING

BRITISH
SEPARATED HEADBOARD

LARGE BOARDS FAIRED INTO HULL

ALTERNATIVE

ANGLE IRON FRAME FOR DETACHABLE BOARDS

GAMMONINGS
AMERICAN
IRON STRAP

BRITISH
CHAIN

DOUBLE BOBSTAY

SINGLE BOBSTAY

1869

TOP RAIL PERMANENT   **1860-70**

CARVING ON STEM KNEE

1850ˢ ONWARDS

CARVING ON STEM & CHEEKS

BRITISH

KNIGHT HEADS OPTIONAL

FLAT STRAIGHT BOARDS, HUNG VERTICALLY

CARVING ON THIN BOARDS ON HULL

AMERICAN

CARVING ON CHEEKS

IRON STEM FAIRED INTO HULL

1850 ONWARDS

New York in 1851 by William Webb. Her deck line was very fine, about 30° from the centreline; and with a graceful flare which made her hull lines finer still, 15° at the load waterline, her sheer mouldings swept into an eagle figurehead with wings outspread on each side. To complete the beauty of this stem, all the standing rigging from the bowsprit and jib-boom, such as backstays, guys, shrouds, etc. went through holes in the hull and were set up inside the forecastle, thus eliminating the eyebolts, chainplates, hearts, deadeyes and lanyards which usually marred the bows. She was a large ship, 230 ft long by 43 ft beam. Most of the American clippers then being produced were large compared to their British counterparts.

As a result of the short and narrow stem knee on these later American clippers, the gammoning which held down the bowsprit was altered. The old method, and that still used on British clippers, was to have a long slot in the stem below the bowsprit, through which a chain was passed and lashed around the bowsprit with several turns, each turn crossing the next from forward to aft in a crisscross fashion, and each turn being nailed either to the stem or the bowsprit if of wood. With this arrangement went a single larger chain bobstay from the stem to the bowsprit end. The American knee, however, was weaker in substance to take a slot and chain gammoning which would also be in way of the figurehead, so a strong iron strap was used instead, which was passed over the bowsprit at a point behind the stem line and only its bolts exposed just outside the stem planking. This was not quite as effective in position as the chain gammoning, being nearer the heel of the bowsprit, so it was usual to introduce two bobstays from the stem to help hold down the bowsprit.

Another rising star in the shipbuilding world, Donald McKay, had come down from Nova Scotia in 1826 to work with Brown & Bell and Isaac Webb in New York as a shipwright and no doubt was absorbing the revolutionary developments around him. There were no schools of theoretical naval architecture for merchant shipbuilding at this time, nor for many years later, and the only training to be had was in practical ship-building, mathematics and geometry. It was left to an intelligent and inquisitive mind to use this basic background to best advantage, coupled with practical cumulative experience, which was the path that McKay trod. John Griffiths was one of his teachers. By 1840 he was in a partner-ship at Newburyport, Massachusetts, building and designing a variety of successful craft, until he was persuaded to go to East Boston in 1845 where he commenced building fast packet ships. The shipbuilding industry in Boston was lagging behind that of the enterprising and energetic New Yorkers, one reason being that Boston merchants still insisted on fuller lines for good carrying capacity. Eventually by the 1850s, the renown of the New York built ships was such that Boston had to take up the challenge, and McKay and a younger man, Samuel Pook, were the leading lights in developing the wonderful clippers that sprang up in many yards along the East Coast. McKay's clippers, although keeping to the clean bow as on the later New Yorkers, tended to retain a longer stem knee and featured a form of decorative headboard which was built flush with the hull without exposed timber supports, and looked very handsome.

The American clippers kept to a square transom type of stern much later than the British, although the *Challenge* was built with a large, deep semicircular counter with about four mouldings of concentric diminishing arcs. Many of McKay's sterns were similar.

The great length of these clippers brought about problems of longitudinal strength which were countered by making the outer keels and inner keelsons of considerable size. Internally, the keelsons were built up of enormous timbers laid side by side and extending upwards also, to such a height that they resembled longitudinal bulkheads. Together with large wooden knees from the centreline pillars, and at the sides also, the space lost contributed much to making these ships uneconomical in later years. Their bulwarks, which in normal shipbuilding practice are not designed as a strength factor, in this case were built high and exceptionally strong, the uppermost rails being heavy solid timber (clamps) from end to end, and the planksheers and waterways also of great sectional area. By comparison, the British style of bulwarks was flimsy, and whole sections were often swept away, although they were normally adequate for their job. Bulwarks, both British and American, often had more sheer forward than the deck. The much deeper keels of the American ships, although primarily for strength, contributed resistance to lateral drift or leeway.

In addition to these precautions for resisting bending strains, the *Challenge* was reputed to be the first American vessel to use diagonal iron plate straps across the outer face of the frames and under the planking.

One of the most significant changes which the refined bows of the clipper ship brought about, however, was in the sheer. This curvature, like an arc of large radius, had from earliest times been set with its tangential point to a level line some distance forward of amidships, which resulted in the poop being higher than the bow at deck level. With the sharper bow, however, and its tendency to sink deeper into a sea, the fore end of the ship needed to be increased in height and this was achieved by first bringing the tangential point to the middle length and eventually well aft of it. The actual amount of curvature was about the same as before, but the bow was higher than the poop, which radically changed the whole aspect of ships such that at a distance it was apparent even if the fullness or slimness was not.

This is most noticeable in films of old sea classics, where necessity has

DEVELOPMENT *of the* UPPER STERN

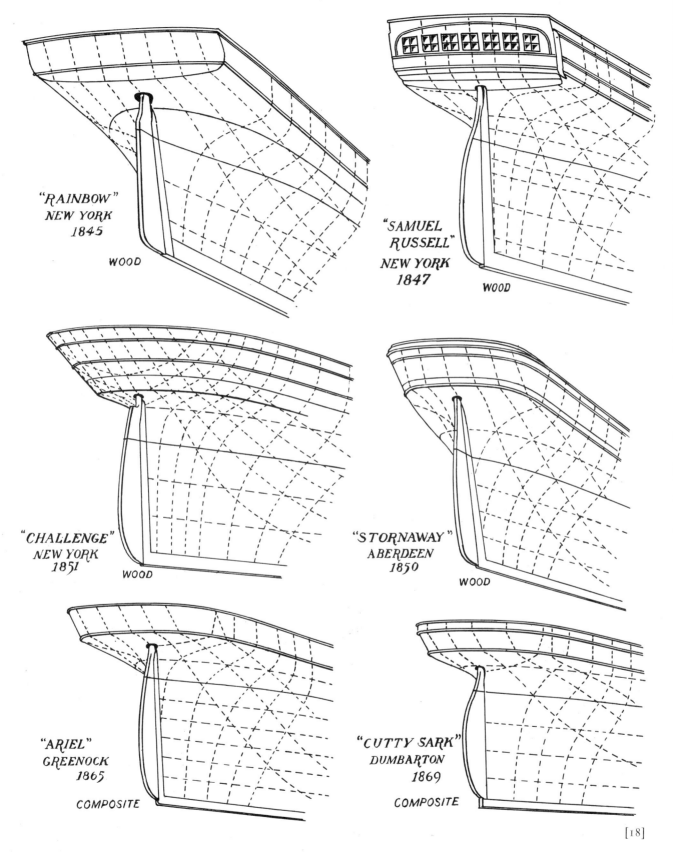

"RAINBOW"
NEW YORK
1845

WOOD

"SAMUEL
RUSSELL"
NEW YORK
1847

WOOD

"CHALLENGE"
NEW YORK
1851

WOOD

"STORNAWAY"
ABERDEEN
1850

WOOD

"ARIEL"
GREENOCK
1865

COMPOSITE

"CUTTY SARK"
DUMBARTON
1869

COMPOSITE

demanded the use of a modern sailing ship hull faked up with a high old-fashioned poop. The original sheer lines can still be seen, which give the old-timer the awkward appearance of squatting by the stern.

The building of true clipper ships in America covered only a short period, approximately from 1845 to 1860, after which time the need for their extreme slim lines no longer existed, and in the following years the sailing ships built were much reduced in rig and capable of carrying a more economical cargo with fuller lines.

In Britain, meanwhile, a parallel development had been going on, in which the change in tonnage assessment in 1836 while encouraging a better form of ship with less draft also allowed inventive minds to gain an advantage by increasing the length above the waterline, particularly in the bow, which gave a slight increase in capacity without increasing taxable tonnage, as against a ship with a straight stem. This elongation of the upper stem, introduced in 1839 on wooden ships by Halls of Aberdeen, was known as the Aberdeen bow and was incorporated in a schooner called the *Scottish Maid* which attracted much attention among the owners of the prospective tea clippers.

It was essentially similar to the bow which the Americans introduced. In itself, it did not make a fast ship under moderate conditions of weather. The advantage lay in the ability to drive harder into rising seas without the sudden check and shock which a full-bowed ship encountered. The old timers had to reduce sail to prevent damage to the fabric of the ship, whereas the clippers could carry on much longer until they too reached a point where the whole stem would bury itself and sail would have to be reduced and the course altered.

As to who was responsible for first introducing this refined bow, both above and below the waterline, it is difficult to say. References to it are usually confined to its evolution in wooden ships. But the development of iron ships must also be taken into account, and power driven hulls. Here the evolution arose from more practical structural reasons. The manufacture and shaping of iron plates leads to a straighter and sharper form of bow, the easiest termination being a straight upright stem. If for appearance it had been desired to keep the overhanging concave curve of stem with the ease of construction of the straight termination of plates, the overhanging projection would have to be carried on in a thin flat plate the same thickness as the plate keel, which would not be a practical proposition. Therefore the upper stem plating was shaped to extend to the curved stem bar, thus arriving at the same result as the wooden stem in both the American and Aberdeen bow. The full development of this can be seen on drawing (15) with the *Lord of the Isles* of 1853, an iron tea clipper which probably derived her form from steamships, a form which persisted until the later days of the sailing ship with varying degrees of fullness. One disadvantage of these early Aberdeen clippers was insufficient sheer forward, which was also the case with the Clyde-built *Lord of the Isles* which had hardly any sheer for her full length, probably as a result of the economical desire to cut the plates as little as possible. This could result in men being swept off the forecastle when nose-diving, a fault which the American ships with their high freeboard and great sheer forward avoided. The fine-bowed steamships were not as subject to this nose-diving, or at least could avoid it, as they did not depend on the wind for the course they set relative to the seas. Some of the best all-round clippers had the underwater body slightly full towards the forefoot to give extra buoyancy and resist the downward plunge.

The after ends of the clippers were also subject to much experimentation in their form below and above the waterline both for speed and sea-worthiness. A good clean run, if carried too far forward, could result in the form above the waterline being too fine also, and the consequent lack of buoyancy result in a following sea engulfing the stern before it had sufficient lift to rise out of it. A notable ship with this tendency was the *Ariel* built by Steele's of Greenock in 1865. If handled carefully, the slimness of her stern could be offset somewhat by shortening sail on the mizzenmast when there was any danger of being pooped. However, there were a number of occasions when she was pooped, and after her disappearance in 1872 it was conjectured that following seas had washed away her helmsman, causing her to broach and founder. The illustration (19) of this possible occurrence will give some idea of the dangers to which a number of Steele's vessels were subject, even if the incident itself is in doubt.

The small, round counter with slight overhang favoured by many clippers was graceful, but provided little help in these circumstances. The heavier counters and transoms on the American ships were not so graceful, but had a similar effect as the bell bow in providing extra lift when required(18). The stern of the *Cutty Sark*, as can be seen today, has a certain amount of fullness under the counter which, while not truly graceful, was no doubt deliberately designed on the experience of her predecessors, although at her other extreme, her knife-like bow and lack of flare resulted in some nose-dives and loss of life.

The years between 1850 and 1870 saw great experimentation in designing the lines of the clippers, of which the evolution of the bow and stern as just outlined was an important part but had to be considered in conjunction with numerous other factors. In the extreme form, there was no parallel body in the middle, and the point of maximum beam varied from amidships to a point either forward or aft of it. Earlier in the century the generality of French designs was to have a flat floor or bottom with a sharp hollow underwater fore body and full after body. Swedish builders

19 The probable fate of the *Ariel* in 1872

(in the forefront of theoretical design) gave a rising floor, a full fore body, and a fine after body, which was the British tendency also. The best clippers had a moderate rise of floor, an easy round of bilge, and the fore and after bodies equally balanced.

The fineness of the extremities of the clippers was such that they could be easily depressed by the addition of little weight. This was taken advantage of, when loading tea, by moving portable weights in boxes along the deck to give a slight trim by the stern. It was long considered that a ship sailed better when trimmed by the stern, and as during the voyage provisions stowed in the after part and fresh water in after tanks would be consumed, this loss of weight could be compensated by the additional weights in the boxes. Tea chests were sometimes stowed (illegally) in the after accommodation.

The fineness of the underwater body could be carried too far in the interests of speed, resulting in instability. The famous *Leander* was at fault in this respect as she needed so much ballast that a full cargo of tea could not be stowed before the ship was down to her marks.

The development of the upper stem in the British clippers closely paralleled the American style, on the wooden and composite hull. After the planked-in, overhanging, Aberdeen type bow, the termination of the bow planking was straightened out to meet the side of the stem in a slightly raking straight line or gentle curve, with the forecastle deck line considerably fined down to a very light hollow flare or straight vee'd section. The long projecting upper stem knees with ornamental side cheeks and headboards with their supporting timbers were too popular to eliminate; a markedly different attitude from that of the Americans, who considered the British tradition as 'old hat'.

However, these headboards were considerably reduced in size and weight and frequently made portable so that once at sea they were unbolted and removed, leaving only a minimum framework. The iron clippers, however, did retain the skin of the ship carried out to the curved stem knee until the last days of the sailing ships, and into modern times in the case of large steam yachts. This style inherited the name 'clipper stem' which we use today whenever it occurs.

One of the greatest difficulties the clipper ship designers faced was the lack of continuing, progressive records on which to build up facts. Naval warship designers could draw on statistics from whole fleets over many years and effect gradual experimental changes to arrive at certain facts, whereas the merchant ship designer had only the ships produced from his own yard on which to prove his theories. Much of what he did was based on instinct guided by intelligent observation, after the elementary facts had been established mathematically.

He was quick to study a successful rival ship in dry dock, although this did not tell all. However, although there was a natural reluctance among owners and builders to impart their hard-earned knowledge to others who were competing, there was a realization that a certain amount of cooperation would benefit all, and the formation of the Institute of Naval Architects in Britain in 1860 was the first step towards this pooling of knowledge.

The grace and beauty of the clipper ships was achieved by men who had an intuitive instinct for good aesthetic taste, influenced by the nature of the material with which they worked. Wood can be carved into grotesque shapes, but it cannot be bent into ugly bends and curves without damaging or rupturing the fibres, and in consequence shipbuilders throughout the ages have used the natural tendencies of the wood to achieve their ends. A vessel such as a Viking ship was not designed beforehand to have beautiful sweeping curves: the shape was the result of the natural bend and twist of the planks with the minimum of cutting away and tapering until the eye judged it to be right.

Great care was taken by designers and draughtsmen in the 19th century who, inheriting old traditions in an unbroken line from the first seagoing vessels, saw to it that their finished products pleased the eye when viewed from any angle. For instance, fair sheer curves on a drawing board for deck at side and deck at centre meeting at a point at the taffrail could turn out an unhappy semicircular or elliptical counter or a square transom, if adjustments were not made to the cambering of the deck at the stern, and in a similar fashion at the bow. They were not always successful, especially with the introduction of metal plates, and occasionally one comes across curved upper and lower mouldings at the knuckles of the counter which were not quite complementary to each other.

In the days when ships' sterns had towering galleries, raking aft and curved both horizontally and vertically yet tapering upwards, it was easy to get a twisted appearance from certain viewpoints if the geometry was not thought out. Contemporary laying-out instructions employed pages of detailed explanations to avoid this.

The larger American clippers with their deep counters and rising levels of two, three, or sometimes four knuckles or mouldings carried on this tradition.

I remember seeing modern vessels with the first raking, round plated stems (soft noses), which did not have the same care taken in their design. From a passing boat the profile of stem would look good, but as one rounded the bow there appeared to be a kink and falling back of the upper part. This was because the rake of the stem did not match the rake or flare of the sides above the hawsepipes, the two having been considered independently.

Some of the old-time drawing office men with whom I was fortunate enough to make a brief acquaintance would speak proudly of laying out a profile for those sleek Atlantic liners of the last century: on balancing the funnel height and diameter against the amount of solid hull above the waterline; the spacing and rake of masts and funnels, and the bands on the funnels. A curved hance was not simply a sweep of the compass, but a gradually increasing bend, roughly described as the profile of the ball of the thumb. All this after the functional design had been decided, which gave the whole a basic truth.

One thing the steamers had in common with their contemporary clipper sisters. Not only did they express power and movement when under way, and readiness for the attack of the sea when it threatened but they also displayed stately content and repose when idle at their moorings or in dock. Their balance was so unlike the present generation of ships plying the Caribbean on their luxury cruises, with their tortured superstructures twisted this way and that in an endeavour to make them look as though they are travelling faster than in fact they are, and denying them any rest at the end of a voyage. If they were moored by the stern anchors it would be more in keeping with their attitude of hounds straining at the leash.

I may add that I have been partly responsible myself for vessels such as these, from the pressures of popular taste, and appreciate the economic necessities involved. One redeeming feature that they have incorporated is the long, sleek, overhanging, curved stem which is almost a direct copy of that on the clipper.

Perfection in sailing clipper ship design was never reached, and could not be reached today on existing knowledge, but what these 19th century designers and craftsmen did produce was truly wonderful, and the images that remain can still excite the imagination and arouse admiration for their beauty and utility in an honourable trade carried on by honourable men.

COMPARISON OF SIZES

The following list of vessels shows the progressive increase in dimensions of British tea clippers, together with some American clippers. At times individual ships were built of exceptional dimensions. Even the largest of them would appear small today in comparison with a moderate sized tramp of say 380 ft. The largest sailing ships of the present century went up to 400 ft in length, while the grain fleet comprising the last of the windjammers in the 1930s averaged 300 ft at 2,400 tons.

BRITISH

Year	Name	L × B × D	Tons	L/B
1848	Sea Witch	121.5 × 26.7 × 16.0	337	4.5
1849	Sea Queen	138.1 × 23.2 × 15.1	372	5.9
1850	Stornoway	157.8 × 28.8 × 17.8	527	5.4
1852	Challenger	174.0 × 32.0 × 20.0	699	5.4
1853	Lord of the Isles	190.0 × 27.6 × 18.5	770	6.9
1854	Vision	170.0 × 27.6 × 18.2	563	6.1
1856	Robin Hood	204.0 × 35.1 × 21.0	852	5.8
1860	Fiery Cross	185.0 × 31.7 × 19.2	695	5.8
1862	Whiteadder	191.3 × 34.0 × 20.6	915	5.6
1863	Taeping	183.7 × 31.1 × 19.9	767	5.9
1865	Sir Lancelot	197.6 × 33.7 × 21.0	886	5.8
1866	Titania	200.0 × 36.0 × 21.0	879	5.5
1867	Leander	210.0 × 35.1 × 28.6	883	5.9
1868	Thermopylae	212.0 × 36.0 × 20.9	948	5.8
1869	Cutty Sark	212.5 × 36.0 × 21.0	921	5.9
1870	Blackadder	216.6 × 35.2 × 20.5	917	6.1

AMERICAN

Year	Name	L × B × D	Tons	L/B
1845	Rainbow	159.0 × 31.1 × 18.4	752	5.1
1846	Sea Witch	170.0 × 33.9 × 19.0	890	5.0
1847	Samuel Russell	173.6 × 34.6 × 19.1	957	5.0
1848	Memnon	170.0 × 36.0 × 21.0	1068	4.7
1849	Oriental	185.0 × 36.0 × 21.0	1003	5.0
1850	Staghound	209.0 × 39.0 × 21.0	1535	5.3
1850	Racehorse	125.0 × 30.0 × 16.0	530	4.1
1851	Swordfish	169.5 × 36.5 × 20.0	1036	4.6
1851	Flying Fish	207.0 × 39.6 × 22.0	1505	5.2
1851	Flying Cloud	229.0 × 40.8 × 21.5	1793	5.6
1851	Comet	229.0 × 42.0 × 22.8	1836	5.4
1851	Challenge	230.0 × 43.0 × 26.0	2006	5.3
1852	Bald Eagle	215.6 × 41.1 × 23.5	1703	5.2

Chapter Four

Hull Construction

Although the use of iron for hull construction was tried successfully on small craft very early in the 19th century, the old traditional methods of wooden construction, in which almost all the shipyards and their personnel were well versed, were still considered the best by the merchant ship owners at the time that the first tea clippers were ordered. In North America, wooden construction persisted until quite late in the century, chiefly because the raw material was readily available, and also because of a high import duty on manufactured iron from Europe. America in those days did not have a self-sufficient iron industry.

There were noticeable differences in the construction methods of merchant ships in British and American yards, due mainly to the much greater length of the American clippers and the necessity of counteracting the hogging strains which tended to bend a ship, the upperworks being in tension and the bottom in compression.

Royal Naval designers had already introduced a series of innovations, such as internal diagonal lattice-work framing over the normal vertical framing, and a solid bottom to resist compression. The latter was achieved by filling in the spacing between the frames either with wooden chocks or planking, up to a point above the round of the bilge. Since the bottom was solid and flush, the bilge water lay above it, and drainage holes were not required in the lower surface of the frames. Although this mode of construction was a great advance, it was not taken up by the merchant ship builders, who kept to the older system of vertical framing spaced out and covered by longitudinal planking, internally (ceiling) as well as externally. The consequent sealing up of heavy timbering was a great inducement to the start of rot. Any wooden structure which has great bulk made up of separate timbers facing onto each other is a source of rot, as clean fresh air cannot circulate. The ancient method of minimizing this was to char the adjoining surfaces beforehand with hot irons, or indulge in the practice of 'worm chasing'. This involved gouging out the surfaces in haphazard grooves, which it was hoped would allow air circulation.

The final solution, however, lay in salting. It was found that wood well soaked beforehand in salt water, or packed with plain salt in any interstices, resisted rot. Lloyd's allowed an extra year of classification if salting was carried out. This was done during construction by completely filling up the gaps between frames, progressively, as the inner limber strakes and ceiling were fitted. The upper surface of deck beams also had a long groove about an inch deep filled with salt before the deck planking was laid, and the same system was applied elsewhere in the timbering. It will be noticed on the drawing of typical wooden hull construction in British-built ships that each frame unit is made up of two sets of timbers or futtocks which although abutted together across the keel gradually open up towards their extremities as their sizes diminish, although the outside

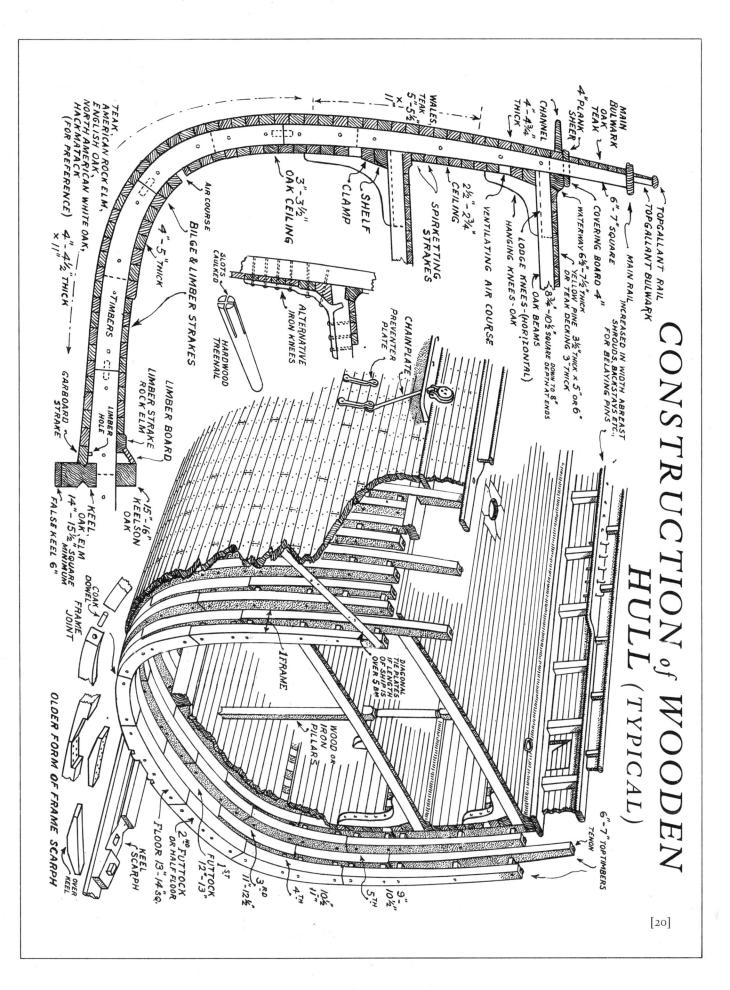

CONSTRUCTION of WOODEN HULL (TYPICAL)

TOPGALLANT RAIL
TOPGALLANT BULWARK
MAIN BULWARK OAK TEAK 6"-7" SQUARE
MAIN RAIL INCREASED IN WIDTH ABREAST SHROUDS, BACKSTAYS ETC., FOR BELAYING PINS
4" PLANK SHEER
COVERING BOARD 4"
WATERWAY 6½"-7½" THICK
YELLOW PINE 3½" THICK × 5" OR 6" OR TEAK DECKING 3" THICK
8¾"-10½" SQUARE DEPTH AT ENDS
DOWN TO 8"
CHANNEL 4"-4¾" THICK
OAK BEAMS
LODGE KNEES (HORIZONTAL)
HANGING KNEES - OAK
2½"-2¾" CEILING
WALES, TEAK 5"-5½" × 11"
3"-3½" OAK CEILING
SPIRKETTING STRAKES
VENTILATING AIR COURSE
SHELF
CLAMP
AIR COURSE
ALTERNATIVE IRON KNEES
SLOTS CAULKED
HARDWOOD TREENAIL
CHAINPLATE
PREVENTER PLATE
BILGE & LIMBER STRAKES
4"-5" THICK
TIMBERS
LIMBER STRAKE ROCK ELM
LIMBER BOARD
LIMBER HOLE
15"-16" OAK, ELM
KEELSON OAK
KEEL OAK 14"-15½" SQUARE MINIMUM
TEAK, AMERICAN ROCK ELM, ENGLISH OAK, NORTH AMERICAN WHITE OAK, HACKMATACK (FOR PREFERENCE) 4"-4½" THICK × 11"
GARBOARD STRAKE
FALSE KEEL 6"
COAK DOWEL
FRAME JOINT
FRAME
DIAGONAL TIE PLATES IF LENGTH OF SHIP IS OVER 5 BM.
WOOD OR IRON PILLARS
6"-7" TOPTIMBERS
TENON
OVER KEEL
KEEL SCARPH
2ND FUTTOCK OR HALF-FLOOR FLOOR 13-14 SQ.
1ST FUTTOCK 12-13
3RD 11-12½
4TH
5TH
9" 10½
10½ 11
OLDER FORM OF FRAME SCARPH

[20]

CONSTRUCTION of WOODEN HULL (TYPICAL AMERICAN)

BULWARKS VARY IN HEIGHT AMIDSHIPS FROM ABOUT 4'6" TO 6'6" INCREASING TOWARDS EXTREMITIES

MONKEY RAIL (TOPGALLANT RAIL)

MAINRAIL 5½" × 20"

2½" BULWARK

6" PLANKSHEER

OAK, HACKMATACK, LOCUST, TOPTIMBERS 6½" MOULDED 10" SIDED

WALES AND TOPSIDES 5½" THICK × 7"

WHITE OAK OR HARD PINE PLANKING

TYPICAL FOR A VESSEL OF ABOUT 200' B.P.

CLAMP

CLAMP

STANCHION

WATERWAY 14" SQUARE

RACK RAIL

SPIRKETTING 9×14"

WATERWAY 15" SQUARE

7" CLAMP OR SHELF

HANGING KNEES HACKMATACK

LODGE KNEE

12"×9"

14" SIDED WATERWAY 15 SQUARE

6" CLAMP

5" LINING

6" × 3½" WHITE PINE

14"SIDED 8½"MOULDED (DEPTH)

3½" HARD PINE DECKING

9" SIDED 14" MOULDED

BEAMS HARD PINE

16" SIDED 16" MOULDED

BEAMS HARD PINE

LIGHT PLANKS

T & G BULWARK PLANKSHEER MOULDING

WAIST MOULDING

WALES

WAIST (WAIST VARIES IN WIDTH)

WALES & FLUSH FINISH

WAIST

MONKEY RAIL

MAIN RAIL WITH RACK RAIL COMBINED

PLANKSHEER

SOLID CLAMP MONKEY RAIL NO STANCHIONS (OR PLANKS AND STANCHIONS)

CLAMP

RACK RAIL

WOOD OR IRON KNEES

DIAGONAL IRON STRAPS 4'0" APART - 4" × ¾" LET INTO FACE OF FRAMES INTRODUCED ABOUT 1851 INTERNAL WOODEN DIAGONALS SOMETIMES FITTED

CEILING GRADUATED FROM 12" AT BILGES TO 5" AT UPPER DECK HARD PINE

7"

7"

12"

4½"

14"

15" SQUARE KEELSONS AND SIDE KEELSONS

4" BOTTOM PLANKS GRADUATED TO 7"GARBOARD

WHITE OAK

FLOORS 12" SIDED 16" MOULDED

SALT PACKED BETWEEN FRAMES

ROCK MAPLE KEEL 3 PIECES 15"SQUARE

KEEL RABBET VARIATION

SEPARATED KEEL SCARPHS IN EACH PIECE

CENTRE KEELSONS 12" SIDED 16" MOULDED

[21]

surfaces remain parallel to each other (20). The purpose of this rather awkward form of construction was originally to allow air circulation, but it also became useful for salting.

There were a number of other systems of forming the framework for a ship; one of the simplest and easiest, both from the constructional point of view and for the geometrical laying off in the mould loft, was that adopted by the majority of American builders and shown in (21). Here two sets of futtock timbers forming one complete frame are all abutted together up to their extremities, the only gap being between each set of frames, which again was filled with salt in the best class of ship. Ships built of teak, incidentally, as many of the English clippers were, did not need salting, as teak has its own resistance to rot.

It will be noticed also that the timbers crossing the top of the keel in the American system do so without any notching out, the rabbet for the bottom planking being at the top of the side of keel. This was also the style in British naval ships. British merchant ships, however, usually took the rabbet out of the side of the keel at a lower point, nearer the middle, which meant that each floor timber or futtock had to be notched out over the keel so that its under surface lay in line with the top edge of the rabbet. One result of this was that the basic keel in British ships projected downwards less than in American construction. Also American ships sought longitudinal strength through additional keel pieces below the basic one, as well as extra keelsons and side keelsons, these latter also helping to stiffen the bottom under the mainmast.

The remaining structural differences between British and American ships were in the latter's much larger waterways, spirketing, bilge and side ceiling, and bulwarks. An additional reason for the greater scantlings of American ships was their use of comparatively softer timber than was used in Europe. Externally, British clippers used a wider plank, up to 11 in. as against an average of 7 in. on American clippers, a difference which is very noticeable in contemporary photographs or paintings. American shipyards also kept to the use of wooden knees for beam ends and elsewhere much later than the British, because of their iron shortage.

The need for extra longitudinal strengthening of long ships, in addition to these features, was still apparent, however, and it was achieved by using the earlier naval practice of diagonal bracing with iron straps over the outer surface of the wooden frames. The straps were let into the frames to provide a flush surface for the outer planking. In the later composite construction the straps were outside the iron frame flange, which meant that the outer planking had to be notched out wherever it crossed a strap.

Another method of construction involving the principle of diagonal bracing was used on a few famous clippers such as the *Vision* and the *Chaa-Sze*. This involved two diagonal layers and one longitudinal layer of external planking, as shown in the drawing of the *Vision*'s structure. This was an exceptionally strong form of construction, very rigid and thoroughly watertight, and used timber of smaller scantlings than the traditional method. The frames were smaller and more widely spaced, and the space between the frames was sometimes filled with an additional layer of planks running vertically, making four skins in all; and a very difficult job to repair (22).

Samuel White of Cowes specialized in this construction for small vessels, as well as for one or two tea clippers, and it had also been used successfully in America on river boats. Usually with this system, for efficient caulking of the garboard to the keel rabbet, two or three strakes from the garboard outwards were normal full-thickness longitudinal planks. The outermost of these strakes was arranged with a rebate which overlapped the ends of the diagonal planks and thus kept them secure against springing out. Similarly the upper ends of the diagonals were secured under a full-thickness longitudinal strake below the sheer strake. The Royal Yacht *Victoria and Albert II* was built in this fashion in 1855. In a few instances the treble thickness of plank did meet the keel with three separate rabbets. Had it not been for the increasingly advantageous use of ironwork in the hull this diagonal system would probably have superseded the traditional wooden hull.

Many of the shipyards devoted to wooden construction lay in remote areas where the majority of the townspeople were employed in the yard and took a great pride in their inherited skills. There was a minimum of shipyard equipment in the way of machinery. Sawing of logs was done by hand with pit saws; blacksmiths or brass finishers were the only metal-working men in the yard; and a long steam chest was the only aid for shaping planks. When one of these yards closed down, there was little left after a while to indicate that there had ever been an establishment capable of building these complicated structures, apart from maybe a small brick-built general office and some wooden shacks. There were no overhead travelling cranes or steam engines to move material about in those days. Sternframes, plating, etc. for iron ships were swung into place by rough tree trunks lashed together into a tripod and equipped with hand-working tackles, a system used well into the 20th century in many yards. Material was moved by hand bogies which were sometimes on rails. A large masting crane or derrick, possibly with a steam winch, would be in the area for general use if the yard did not have one of its own.

With educational facilities no more than a local schoolroom, which, however, taught well the basic three Rs, there was little opportunity for the working man to learn anything beyond his inherited trade. In consequence, although the introduction of iron shipbuilding had been

THE "VISION" OF LIVERPOOL

AN ABERDEEN BUILT CLIPPER
OF 1854 WITH SOME
UNUSUAL FEATURES
170' x 27.6' x 18.2'
563 TONS (NEW MEASURE)

LEADED GLASS PANES TO POOP
& SKYLIGHT

PILLAR BOX TYPE
STEERING
GEAR

CUT-AWAY VIEW SHOWING
DIAGONAL CONSTRUCTION

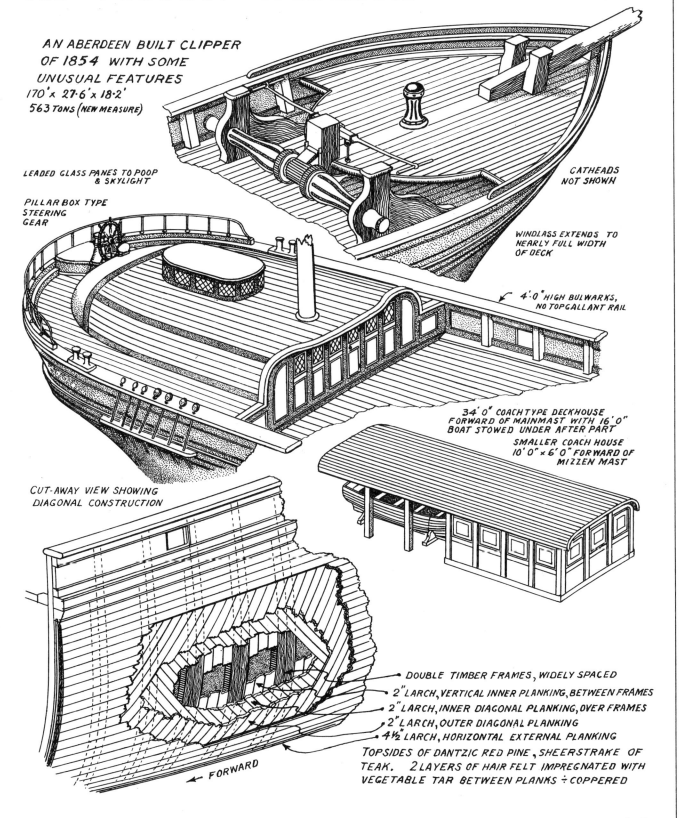

CATHEADS
NOT SHOWN

WINDLASS EXTENDS TO
NEARLY FULL WIDTH
OF DECK

4'-0" HIGH BULWARKS,
NO TOPGALLANT RAIL

34'-0" COACH TYPE DECKHOUSE
FORWARD OF MAINMAST WITH 16'-0"
BOAT STOWED UNDER AFTER PART
SMALLER COACH HOUSE
10'-0" x 6'-0" FORWARD OF
MIZZEN MAST

DOUBLE TIMBER FRAMES, WIDELY SPACED
2" LARCH, VERTICAL INNER PLANKING, BETWEEN FRAMES
2" LARCH, INNER DIAGONAL PLANKING, OVER FRAMES
2" LARCH, OUTER DIAGONAL PLANKING
4½" LARCH, HORIZONTAL EXTERNAL PLANKING
TOPSIDES OF DANTZIC RED PINE, SHEERSTRAKE OF
TEAK. 2 LAYERS OF HAIR FELT IMPREGNATED WITH
VEGETABLE TAR BETWEEN PLANKS ÷ COPPERED

← FORWARD

[22]

effected quite early in the 19th century, and its merits had become fairly obvious, many shipyards could not undertake to make iron hulls because of the lack of experience of the workers, who were also naturally reluctant to give up their trade of wooden shipwrighting. Added to this, the ship-yards themselves could not afford the sophisticated power machines necessary for fashioning iron plates and angles, nor did they have the room for them. The prejudice against ironwork was such that even in more populated areas, where personnel could be recruited from other civil engineering fields, some shipbuilders held out against it, and owners perhaps more so.

An example of this is provided by the famous shipbuilder Thomas Royden of Liverpool, whose shipyard was established in 1818 and who by 1863 had built over seventy wooden ships, some of them with engines. In this year, however, when his two sons quoted, against his wish, for the construction of two iron-hulled ships, he said he would quit if they got the order. They did and he did; and the firm went on to build some of the finest and longest-lasting metal-hulled sailing and steamships ever to sail the oceans.

By a curious coincidence, in the same year, 1863, the well known Blackwall frigate builder Richard Green died. Up to the time of his death he had steadfastly refused to build in anything other than teak and oak, and only after his death the firm commenced building iron ships.

However, some far-sighted Scotsmen saw the necessity for starting shipyards from scratch, equipped with the necessary machinery for iron plate and angle work, and with men specially trained for this work alone. The traditional shipwright was still necessary for decks and many parts of the ship's structure and for the lining off and mould loft work. Demarca-tion of work was always a sore point, no man, understandably, being willing to see his traditional function usurped, and it was finally agreed that shipwrights would actually mark out the metalwork and make the templates for it. Demarcation of work was such that, for instance, a plain wooden rail, simply rounded off at the edges, would be a shipwright's job, whereas if the edges were moulded to a fancy shape they would become a ship joiner's work. This may seem to be splitting hairs to those whose job has never been encroached upon, but usually when new methods or materials are introduced into a work procedure, a sensible consultation well beforehand can settle any differences, whereas a sudden presentation of such a situation with a loss in earning power for someone will cause trouble.

Two of the far-sighted Scotsmen mentioned were John Laird, who established a shipyard on Merseyside at Birkenhead, and William Fairburn, whose yard was on the Thames. This was in the 1830s. The banks of these two rivers became the main centres for iron shipbuilding, with the Clyde

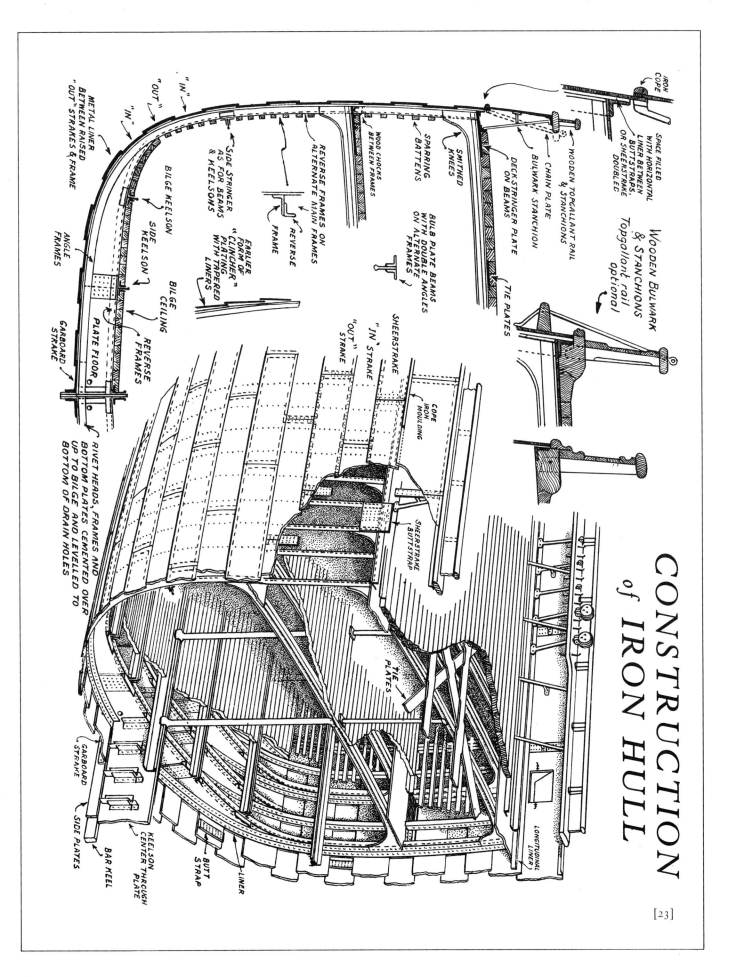

CONSTRUCTION of IRON HULL

[23]

and most of the Northwest coast shipyards following soon after. As early as 1838 an iron sailing ship, the *Ironsides*, had been built in Liverpool, followed intermittently by others. On the Northwest coast a handsome iron schooner, the *Lowca*, was built by a Cumberland iron foundry in 1843 with such enthusiasm that she was practically all iron, masts and rigging as well as hull. She was the first vessel so rigged to round Cape Horn. Wire rigging did not become general on the clippers until the 1860s. American clippers kept to hemp standing rigging until the end of their era.

The earliest iron hull plates were very small by today's standards, no more than 6 ft by 2 ft 6 in. by approximately $\frac{3}{4}$ to $\frac{7}{8}$ in. thick, and with about 18 in. frame spacing; the arrangement of butts was like bricks in a wall (23). By the 1860s the plates had increased in length to a minimum of 9 ft and butt joints were spaced at least one frame space clear of each other. Each strake of plating was still very narrow, between 2 ft 6 in. and 3 ft wide, which meant easier handling in erection and a minimum of shaping. Shaping to the hull form was done by passing the plate between rollers which could be adjusted to vary the amount of curvature at each end without any compound curves. Any compound curves necessitated the plate being furnaced until red hot and then quickly hammered to shape over iron-strapped template formers. As soon as the plate was withdrawn from the furnace, a gang of men attacked it with heavy hammers, like demons from hell, with red-hot sparks flying in all directions. The plate might have to be furnaced a second time before the correct shape was made. This process was expensive and kept to an absolute minimum, usually only two plates being involved, called 'oxter' plates, from their similarity to the armpit, their situation being under the counter just forward of the rudder hole.

The greatest difficulty in early ironwork lay in the bevelling of the outer flange of the angle iron frame. This also had to be done while hot, the bevel being in a twisted form to suit the hull lines, which varied from end to end of the length of frame. All too often this was badly done, being a difficult operation, with the result that the hull plates did not lie truly flush against the flange for tight riveting, and numerous iron strips or liners had to be inserted to fill the gap. Rivet holes were frequently punched too close to the edge of the plate or out of good alignment with each other. These were some of the well-founded reasons why the iron-hulled ships were slow to receive widespread approval, and Lloyd's were slow also in granting them a good class. This lack of approval or classification for a short term of years caused resentment in the Liverpool area as the Merseyside yards did for the most part produce excellent work, and Laird's on the opposite bank of the river were acknowledged to be masters at the craft. As a result, the Liverpool shipowners and builders instituted their own rules and registry for iron ships in 1862 which finally became amalgamated with Lloyd's Register of Shipping, London, in 1885.

Prior to this Lloyd's had instituted rules for iron ship construction in 1855 which were periodically revised in the light of growing experience, but based on the tonnage of the ship as the basis for scantlings, as with wooden ships. However by 1870 the wiser method of using physical dimensions as the criterion was in use, this assessment treating the hull as a girder of known section and length. Up to the early part of the 19th century it had been assumed generally that no good class wooden merchant ships were capable of being built anywhere other than on the Thames, and Lloyd's surveyors were apt to give the country-built craft a very short term of years for classification. Liverpool shipowners bought quite a number of their ships from the Canadian provinces and the United States, these being built of comparatively softer wood than the best British ships, although with increased scantlings to compensate, but these vessels also received poor classification. All this was part of the general irritation which caused Liverpool to work independently of Lloyd's of London, and they had established their own rules and classification for wooden ships back in 1838, which eventually combined with Lloyd's in 1845, their differences over iron ship construction following later, as just mentioned.

The main advantage of the iron hull was the increase in internal volume, the structural members being so very much smaller. Other advantages were that the stem bar, being a continuation of the iron bar keel, was much sharper than the wooden stem, being only about 2 in. thick. The increase in strength and the greater resistance to fire were obvious, but durability remained to be proved. The disadvantages as expressed by the critics, apart from the possibility of poor workmanship such as in riveting, were for the most part biased. It was claimed that the iron hull sweated to the extent that it damaged cargoes, especially in the case of tea. However, in the composite system of construction, which achieved its peak with the tea clippers, the decks were constructed precisely the same as on the iron ships, that is, with open exposed beams bound together at their outer ends by stringer plates and with longitudinal and diagonal tie plates elsewhere, all being covered by the deck planking.

The iron-plated hull side could induce some sweating, but this would drain down between the frames and behind the sparring battens clear of any cargo. Hold ventilators of the cowl type were also introduced on metal hulled ships some time before they were used on wooden ships, and considerably alleviated the sweating problem. The wholly wooden hull also had its disadvantages, as the strain from the rigging when heeled over opened up side and deck seams and caused leakage of salt water; the moisture from sweating was at least distilled water.

Another stated disadvantage of the iron hull was the fouling of the bottom by marine growth and consequent reduction in speed, although the greater problem of damage by teredo worms was eliminated. The fouling and worm problem had been overcome on the wooden bottoms by copper sheathing, which was also found by experimentation to have slightly less resistance to speed than a painted surface. But experiments had also been carried out with a variety of bottom paint compositions to resist corrosion as well as marine growth fouling, which was chiefly seaweed and barnacles. These paints contained poisonous chemicals and were more or less successful. In one reported case, two iron steamships sent to India in the 1840s kept perfectly clean bottoms after nine months' service, and similar reports appear regarding iron ships from different parts of the world. One of the secrets of successful bottom painting, as it is today, lay in application on a clean, dry surface, a condition not easily met in the British climate. But the successful paints and solutions in those days, before the cult of advertising as we know it, probably were not sufficiently publicized to overcome the foul iron bottom objection. A neglected ship could acquire 8 in. or more of barnacles, and trailing seaweed several feet in length.

The smooth golden or copper coloured bottoms one sometimes sees on builders' models of iron steamships in museums represent these early bottom compositions, which used powdered copper as a base. The pink bottoms, also popular and quite successful, were simple mixes basically of tallow and red lead. Pale green bottoms were copper arsenate based paints, which on models are not to be confused with the green colour modelmakers used to imitate copper sheathing.

While iron ships were inexorably superseding wooden ones, and supplies of good timber were becoming more difficult to obtain, there appeared on the scene a compromise which for a brief period was to produce the finest tea clippers ever built. These were the composite ships, which had a basic skeleton of iron covered by a wooden skin. Many combinations of iron with wood skin structure had been tried in the early part of the 19th century; also iron beam knees, then iron beams, and next iron beams and iron upper frames, but all with wooden skins which could also take the copper sheathing so much in favour for speed.

It was this latter fact which provided some shipowners with an excuse not to go all out for an iron hull, which of course could not take copper sheathing. Speed of building and cost also often influenced the decision. Those shipbuilders whose yards could not be economically converted to build complete iron hulls for the reasons mentioned earlier were also glad to take up the challenge.

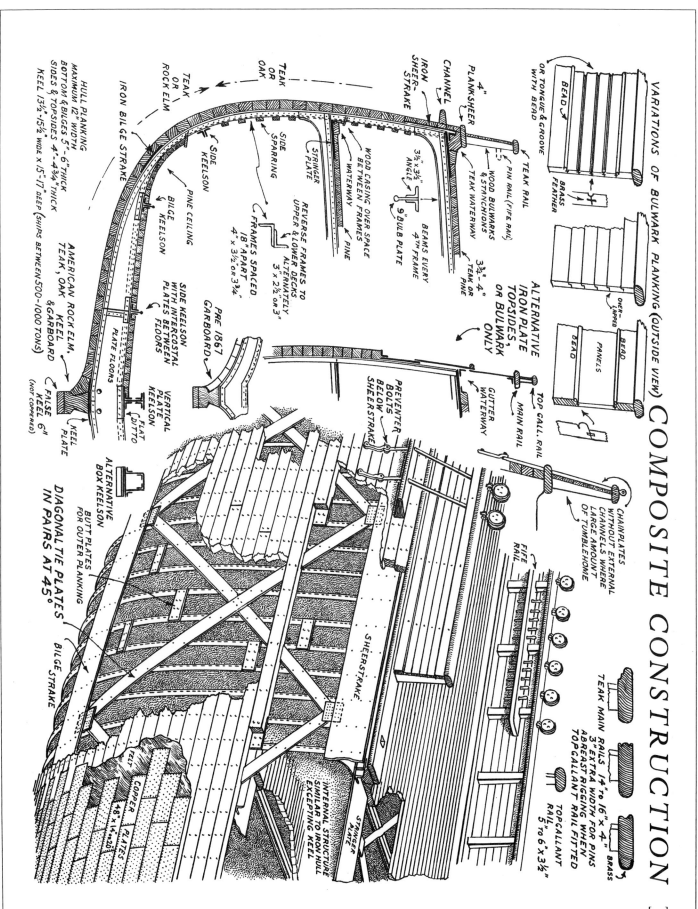

VARIATIONS OF BULWARK PLANKING (OUTSIDE VIEW)

COMPOSITE CONSTRUCTION

OR TONGUE & GROOVE WITH BEAD

BEAD
BRASS
FEATHER

OVER-LAPPED
BEAD
PANELS
BEAD

ALTERNATIVE IRON PLATE TOPSIDES, OR BULWARK ONLY

TEAK RAIL
PIN RAIL (FIFE RAIL)
WOOD BULWARKS & STANCHIONS
TEAK WATERWAY
PLANKSHEER
4"
IRON SHEER-STRAKE
CHANNEL
3½" × 3½" ANGLE
9" BULB PLATE
BEAMS EVERY 4TH FRAME
3½"-4"
TEAK OR PINE
TEAK OR PINE
WOOD CASING OVER SPACE BETWEEN FRAMES
WATERWAY
PINE
STRINGER PLATE
SIDE SPARRING
REVERSE FRAMES TO UPPER & LOWER DECKS ALTERNATELY 3 × 2½ OR 3"
SIDE KEELSON
FRAMES SPACED 18" APART 4" × 3½"
PINE CEILING
BILGE KEELSON
SIDE KEELSON WITH INTERCOSTAL PLATES BETWEEN FLOORS
PRE 1867 GARBOARD
VERTICAL PLATE KEELSON
PLATE FLOORS
FLAT DITTO
ALTERNATIVE BOX KEELSON
KEEL PLATE
FALSE KEEL 6" (NOT COPPERED)

TOP GALL. RAIL
MAIN RAIL
GUTTER WATERWAY
PREVENTER BOLTS BELOW SHEERSTRAKE
CHAINPLATES WITHOUT EXTERNAL CHANNELS WHERE LARGE AMOUNT OF TUMBLEHOME
FIFE RAIL

TEAK MAIN RAILS 14" TO 16" × 4". 3" EXTRA WIDTH FOR PINS ABREAST RIGGING WHEN TOPGALLANT RAIL FITTED
TOPGALLANT RAIL 5" TO 6" × 3½"
BRASS

SHEERSTRAKE

BUTT PLATES FOR OUTER PLANKING

DIAGONAL TIE PLATES IN PAIRS AT 45°

BILGE STRAKE

INTERNAL STRUCTURE SIMILAR TO IRON HULL EXCEPTING KEEL

STRINGER PLATE

FEET
COPPER PLATES +8 × 14 = 20

TEAK OR OAK
TEAK OR ROCK ELM
IRON BILGE STRAKE

HULL PLANKING MAXIMUM 12" WIDTH BOTTOM & BILGES 5"-6" THICK SIDES & TOPSIDES 4"-4¾" THICK KEEL 13½"-15½" WIDE × 15-17" DEEP (SHIPS BETWEEN 500-1000 TONS)

AMERICAN ROCK ELM, TEAK, OAK KEEL & GARBOARD

[24]

Among the many ingenious ways of planking externally over an iron framework, that of a Mr Jordan of Liverpool, invented in 1849, was the best, and with minor changes was the system used for the majority of the more famous tea clippers up to the end of this era in Britain (America never went in for composite building).

The drawing of composite construction shows the final development of this system (24). A number of schooners, barques and ships were built in Liverpool in this manner in the decade following the invention, and the first tea clipper to be built under the same patent was the *Taeping* by Robert Steele on the Clyde in 1863.

Another system closely following normal wooden construction was MacLaine's, whereby angle iron frames had a complete iron-plated skin on the inner sides like an iron hull turned inside out. Between these exposed frames, which were spaced in pairs, additional wooden frames were bolted, to which a longitudinally planked wooden skin was bolted. This was a wasteful arrangement which did not survive very long.

The only other system which could compete with Jordan's was that introduced by Thomas Bilbe on the Thames in 1856. Iron channel bar frames were used with the two flanges pointing outboard. The bosoms of these channels were filled with wooden chocks or frames, usually teak, standing proud of the flanges and on which the external planking was bolted. The bolts passed through the webs of the frames, through enlarged holes so as not to touch the frame, and the inner end of each bolt was then tightened up on the inner wooden ceiling. Two tea clippers built by Bilbe in this fashion were the *Red Riding Hood* (1857) and the *Lauderdale* (1858), the latter having the diagonal system of external planking also.

In all these systems the keel, stem, sternpost, and usually the waterways were of wood, with the side framing, floors, keelsons, stringers, sheerstrake, deck beams, diagonal straps and deck tie plates of iron. The greatest problem was to avoid contact between the copper sheathing and any ferrous metal where salt water could touch both and set up an electrolytic action. For this reason Lloyd's suggested that the bolt fastenings of the external planking be made of yellow metal or copper. If of iron, preferably galvanized, the external heads had to be sunk below the face of the planks and covered with a wooden dowel or cement mix and in addition covered with a minimum of $1\frac{1}{4}$ in. of wood sheathing on top of hair felt. These latter measures could considerably alter the lines of the hull and the displacement. Internally, with the Jordan system, the bolts were tightened up directly on the iron frames, but if of copper or yellow metal they were insulated to some extent by a coating of guttapercha or red oxide paint. Despite the fact that bilge or condensed water could make contact with these fastenings, they seem to have successfully stood the test, as those on the existing *Cutty Sark* bear testimony.

BOW and STERN CONSTRUCTION

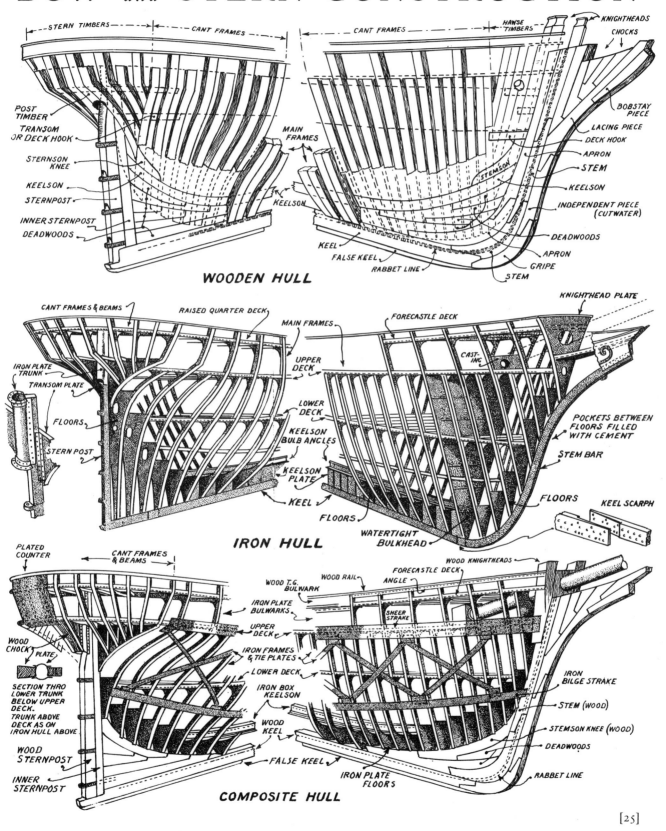

WOODEN HULL

Stern side labels: STERN TIMBERS, CANT FRAMES, POST TIMBER, TRANSOM OR DECK HOOK, STERNSON KNEE, KEELSON, STERNPOST, INNER STERNPOST, DEADWOODS, MAIN FRAMES, KEELSON

Bow side labels: CANT FRAMES, HAWSE TIMBERS, KNIGHTHEADS, CHOCKS, BOBSTAY PIECE, LACING PIECE, DECK HOOK, APRON, STEM, KEELSON, INDEPENDENT PIECE (CUTWATER), DEADWOODS, APRON, GRIPE, STEM, STEMSON, KEEL, FALSE KEEL, RABBET LINE

IRON HULL

Stern side labels: CANT FRAMES & BEAMS, RAISED QUARTER DECK, MAIN FRAMES, UPPER DECK, IRON PLATE TRUNK, TRANSOM PLATE, FLOORS, STERN POST, LOWER DECK, KEELSON BULB ANGLES, KEELSON PLATE, KEEL, FLOORS

Bow side labels: FORECASTLE DECK, KNIGHTHEAD PLATE, CASTING, POCKETS BETWEEN FLOORS FILLED WITH CEMENT, STEM BAR, FLOORS, WATERTIGHT BULKHEAD, KEEL SCARPH

COMPOSITE HULL

Stern side labels: PLATED COUNTER, CANT FRAMES & BEAMS, WOOD CHOCK, PLATE, SECTION THRO LOWER TRUNK BELOW UPPER DECK. TRUNK ABOVE DECK AS ON IRON HULL ABOVE, WOOD STERNPOST, INNER STERNPOST

Bow side labels: WOOD T.G. BULWARK, WOOD RAIL, WOOD KNIGHTHEADS, FORECASTLE DECK, ANGLE, IRON PLATE BULWARKS, SHEER STRAKE, UPPER DECK, IRON FRAMES & TIE PLATES, LOWER DECK, IRON BOX KEELSON, WOOD KEEL, FALSE KEEL, IRON PLATE FLOORS, IRON BILGE STRAKE, STEM (WOOD), STEMSON KNEE (WOOD), DEADWOODS, RABBET LINE

[25]

The ironwork in the composite construction was such that some of the older yards could reasonably tackle it. The only flat plates of any size or awkward shape were the floor plates. The angle irons were bent and bevelled to shape without the necessity of any heavy machinery, and the tie plates, sheerstrakes etc. could be fitted almost as supplied by the iron foundry, leaving only the floor plates with shaped contours to present any difficulty, especially if the edges were curved convex or concave. One way this was done in a poorly equipped yard was to punch or drill a series of overlapping holes to perforate the edge almost like a postage stamp.

The beam knees were smithed out as part of the beam plate itself, this being done by a new style of craftsman known as the anglesmith, who was rightly as proud of his work as the master shipwright. The best of them could smith an angle bar into complicated bends so that it could cross another angle bar at right angles and fit tight and snug around it, needing only a light caulking to become watertight. Both the anglesmiths and platers developed high degrees of skill and started a tradition as good as that of the old-time shipwrights, each of them having his distinctive clothing as suited his trade; the shipwrights with their short collarless jackets and rough blue serge trousers with long rule pocket, and the ironworkers with their moleskin trousers, often pipeclayed for Monday mornings and covered with a thick moleskin or leather apron, to handle plates against their thighs, and with the inevitable sweat-rag of thick red flannel or cotton tow hanging from a back pocket.

Excepting the few instances where a composite ship was produced at an owner's request in an established ironworking shipyard, the finish of the ironwork on the composite ships was not quite up to the standards of the yards with better equipment. But the finish of the timber was of the highest class. Teak, oak and elm were chiefly used. The former wood, introduced from the East earlier in the century, was a great boon to British shipbuilders given the perpetual scarcity of good home-grown woods. English oak was always the superior wood, although it did have a bad effect on iron fastenings, but the best elm, used where it would remain continuously wet, was North American.

American clippers were often described as being built of softwood, which was not true, although their timbers were softer by comparison to the best British ships. American oak, rock maple, hackmatack (a type of larch), locust, hard pine and other native American woods were used in their construction, and although not classed by Lloyd's for the same number of years as the teak or English oak, it was chiefly by reason of their tendency for incipient rot from insufficient seasoning. The softwood (yellow pine) ships from the Canadian Maritime Provinces were produced later in the century to satisfy a growing demand for such timber in domestic building in England, many of the ships themselves being rather hastily constructed with the intention of their being dismantled and sold along with their deck cargoes of wood on arrival in England. References to yellow pine in the British context indicate what is known in America as white pine, which is a beautiful soft pale yellow timber used for pattern making. Its use for ships' decks could only be where there was to be no handling of any heavy sharp-cornered hatch webs or deck cargoes.

A noticeable feature about the wood, iron or composite ship is the attachment of the rigging to the ship's side. The wooden ships had their shrouds, backstays etc. led outboard and attached to the hull over projecting channels, with deadeyes and lanyards from chainplates. The earliest iron ships also had this arrangement. The later iron clippers with plate bulwarks and waterways started the system of attaching the rigging inboard from iron rods (chainplates) attached to the inside lower part of the bulwark, still with deadeyes. If the iron hull had wooden bulwarks and waterways, which was sometimes the case for good appearance, the channels and outboard attachments would apply. Composite ships also, with iron bulwarks, would have the rigging chainplates inboard, and outboard channels if wooden bulwarks. In the latter case, the preventer bolts and chainplate bolts would be fastened through the hull at a depth below the sheerstrake so as not to pierce and weaken it.

The drawings showing the various forms of construction also indicate different methods of planking up the bulwarks, which were a noticeable feature, especially if the seams were beaded or bevelled, as with many American ships.

The setting up of rigging with stretching screws instead of deadeyes occurred at a later date than the tea clipper era, although there is an occasional mention of bowsprit rigging being set up with screws around the stem. Iron deadeyes were also used in some instances instead of the usual lignum vitae; naval vessels used elm.

During the last war a friend of mine was chief officer on a troop transport which put into the Falkland Islands. He took a boat's party around the harbour for some relaxation and boarded the hulk of the *Great Britain*, built in 1843, which was lying afloat there at the time. Finding some deadeyes still in place he sent back for the hacksaw, and after sawing through the bolt succeeded in freeing one which was of cast iron, about 12 in. in diameter. For the next two years he carried it around the seven seas through strafings and bombings until he finally berthed at his home port of London. Leaving the dock with the weighty deadeye in his luggage, he waited an unconscionable time without a bus or taxi appearing, until in disgust he deposited his burden on the kerbstone and hiked into town. So if any resident of East Ham has a large cast iron bun with three holes . . .

In the sectional view of the keel and floor plate on the drawing of

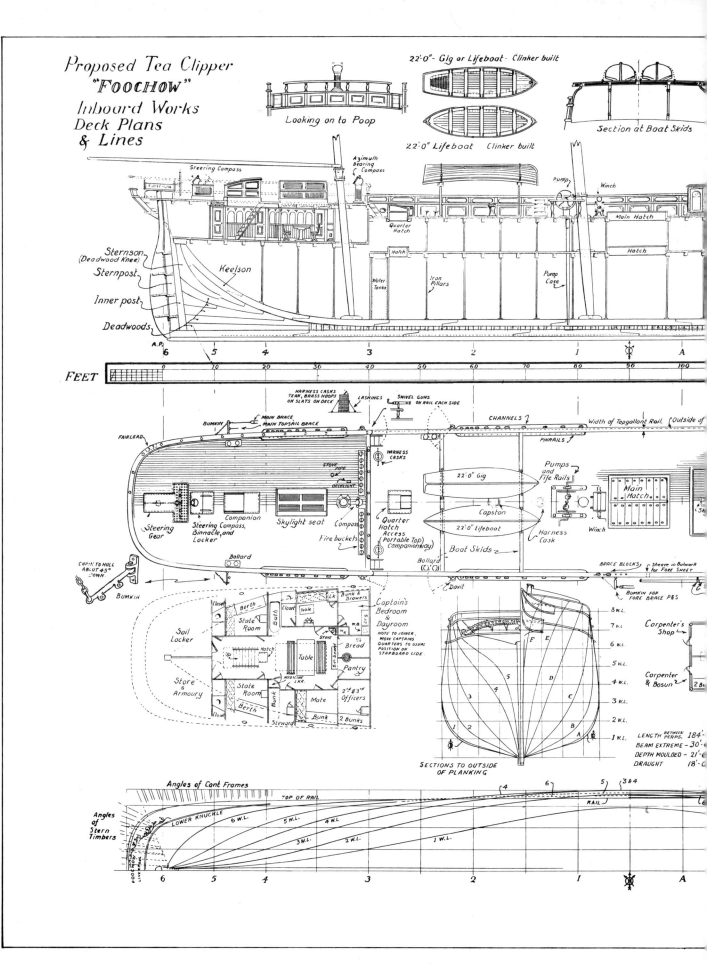

Proposed Tea Clipper
"FOOCHOW"
Inboard Works
Deck Plans
& Lines

22'-0"- Gig or Lifeboat - Clinker built

Looking on to Poop

22'-0" Lifeboat   Clinker built

Section at Boat Skids

Steering Compass

Azimuth Bearing Compass

Pump

Winch

Main Hatch

Quarter Hatch

Hatch

Sternson (Deadwood Knee)

Sternpost.

Inner post.

Deadwoods.

Keelson

Water Tanks

Iron Pillars

Pump Case

A.P. 6   5   4   3   2   1   A

FEET   0   10   20   30   40   50   60   70   80   90   100

HARNESS CASKS TEAK, BRASS HOOPS ON SLATS ON DECK

LASHINGS

SWIVEL GUNS ON RAIL EACH SIDE

CHANNELS

Width of Topgallant Rail. (Outside of

MAIN BRACE
MAIN TOPSAIL BRACE

BUMKIN

PINRAILS

FAIRLEAD

HARNESS CASKS

Pumps and Fife Rails

STOVE PIPE

DECKLIGHT

22'-0" Gig

Main Hatch

Steering Gear

Steering Compass, Binnacle, and Locker

Companion

Skylight seat

Compass

Quarter Hatch Access Portable Top Companionway

Capston

22'-0" Lifeboat

Harness Cask

Winch

Fire buckets

CHAIN TO HULL ABOUT 45° DOWN

BUMKIN

Bollard

Bollard (O.'O)

Boat Skids

Davit

BRACE BLOCKS

Sheave in Bulwark for Fore Sheet

BUMKIN for FORE BRACE P&S

Closet

Berth

State Room

Bath

Closet

Table

Lk

Bunk & Drawers

Lk

Captain's Bedroom & Dayroom

NOTE TO JOINER. MOVE CAPTAINS QUARTERS TO USUAL POSITION ON STARBOARD SIDE.

3 W.L.

7 W.L.

Carpenter's Shop

Sail Locker

W.B. CS

STOVE

Bread

6 W.L.

Store & Armoury

Hatch

Up.

Table

SC Lkrs

Medicine LKR.

Pantry

5 W.L.

4 W.L.

Carpenter & Bosun

2 B

State Room

Berth

Bunk

Mate

Bunk

2nd & 3rd Officers

3 W.L.

2 W.L.

Closet

Steward

2 Bunks

1 W.L.

SECTIONS TO OUTSIDE OF PLANKING

LENGTH BETWEEN PERPS. 184'-
BEAM EXTREME - 30'-
DEPTH MOULDED - 21'-6
DRAUGHT   18'-0

Angles of Cant Frames

TOP OF RAIL

4   6   5   3 & 4

RAIL

Angles of Stern Timbers

LOWER KNUCKLE

6 W.L.

5 W.L.

4 W.L.

3 W.L.

2 W.L.

1 W.L.

6   5   4   3   2   1   A

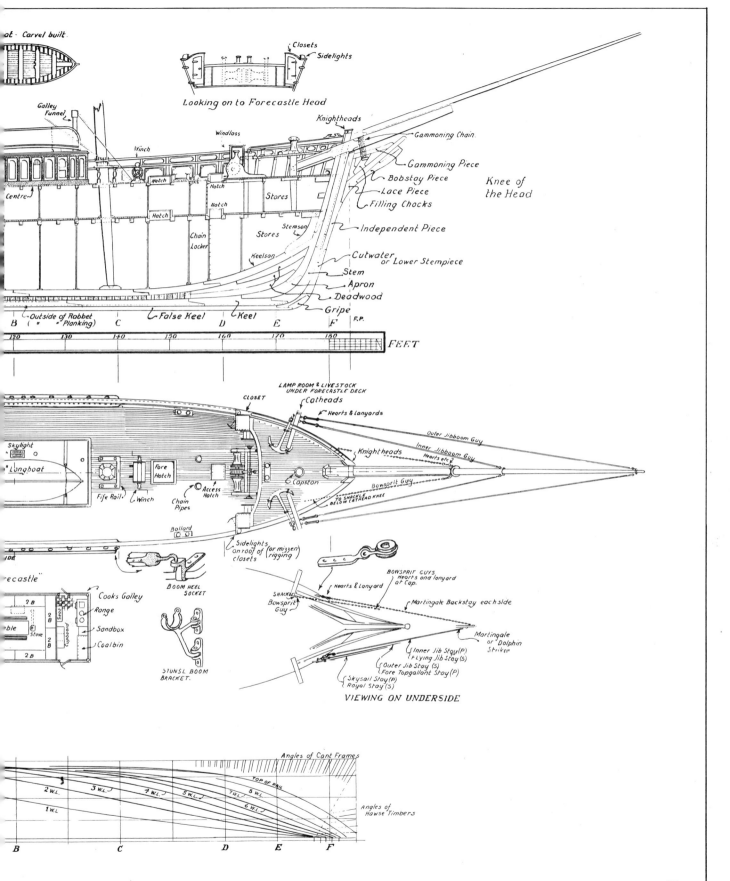

at · Carvel built.

Looking on to Forecastle Head

Closets
Sidelights

Galley Funnel
Winch
Windlass
Knightheads
Gammoning Chain.
Gammoning Piece
Bobstay Piece
Lace Piece
Filling Chocks
Centre
Hatch
Hatch
Hatch
Stores
Stores
Stemson
Chain Locker
Keelson
Independent Piece
Knee of the Head
Cutwater or Lower Stempiece
Stem
Apron
Deadwood
Gripe
Outside of Rabbet (" " Planking)
False Keel
Keel
B   C   D   E   F   F.P.
120   130   140   150   160   170   180
FEET

LAMP ROOM & LIVESTOCK UNDER FORECASTLE DECK
CLOSET
Catheads
Hearts & Lanyards
Outer Jibboom Guy
Inner Jibboom Guy
Hearts etc
Knightheads
Skylight
"Longboat"
Fore Hatch
Access Hatch
Fife Rail
Winch
Chain Pipes
Capston
Bowsprit Guy
TO SHACKLE BELOW CATHEAD KNEE
Bollard
Sidelights on roof of (or mizzen closets rigging)

BOOM HEEL SOCKET
Cooks Galley
Range
Sandbox
Coalbin
2 B
Seat
Stove
Cupboard
2 B
2 B
2 B
ble

STUNS'L BOOM BRACKET.

BOWSPRIT GUYS
Hearts and lanyard at Cap.
SHACKLE
Bowsprit Guy
Hearts & Lanyard
Martingale Backstay each side
Martingale or Dolphin Striker
Inner Jib Stay (P)
Flying Jib Stay (S)
Outer Jib Stay (S)
Fore Topgallant Stay (P)
Skysail Stay (P)
Royal Stay (S)

VIEWING ON UNDERSIDE

Angles of Cant Frames
TOP OF RAIL
2 W.L.
3 W.L.
4 W.L.
5 W.L.
7 W.L.
8 W.L.
1 W.L.
6 W.L.
Angles of Hawse Timbers
B   C   D   E   F

Copyright - George F. Campbell M.R.I.N.A.

26

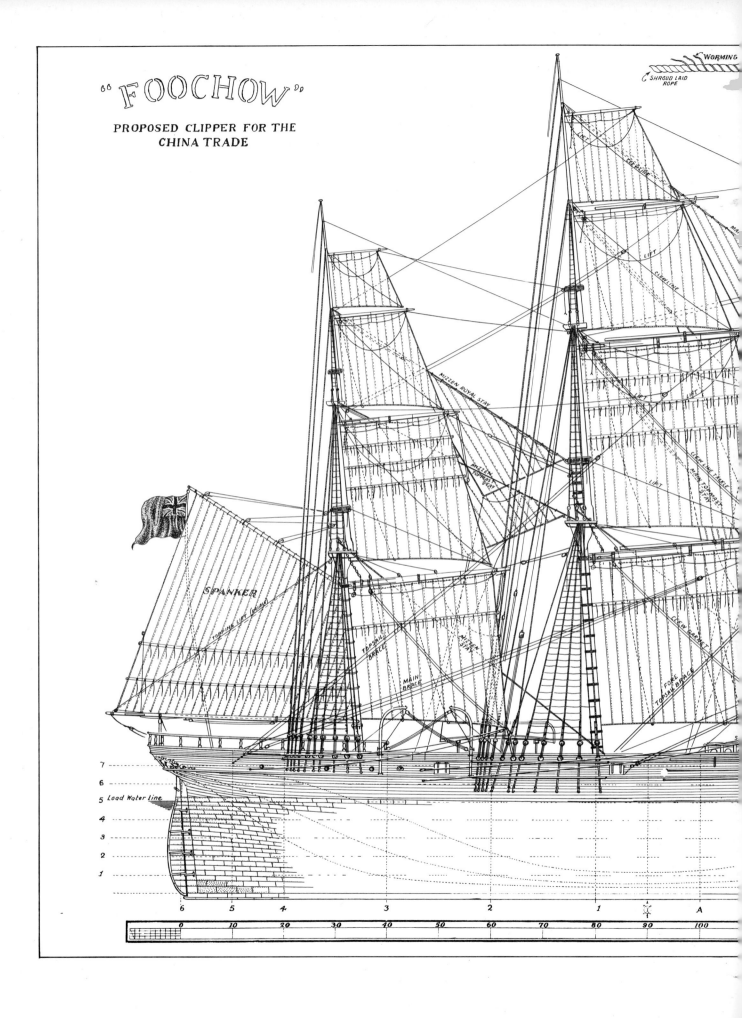

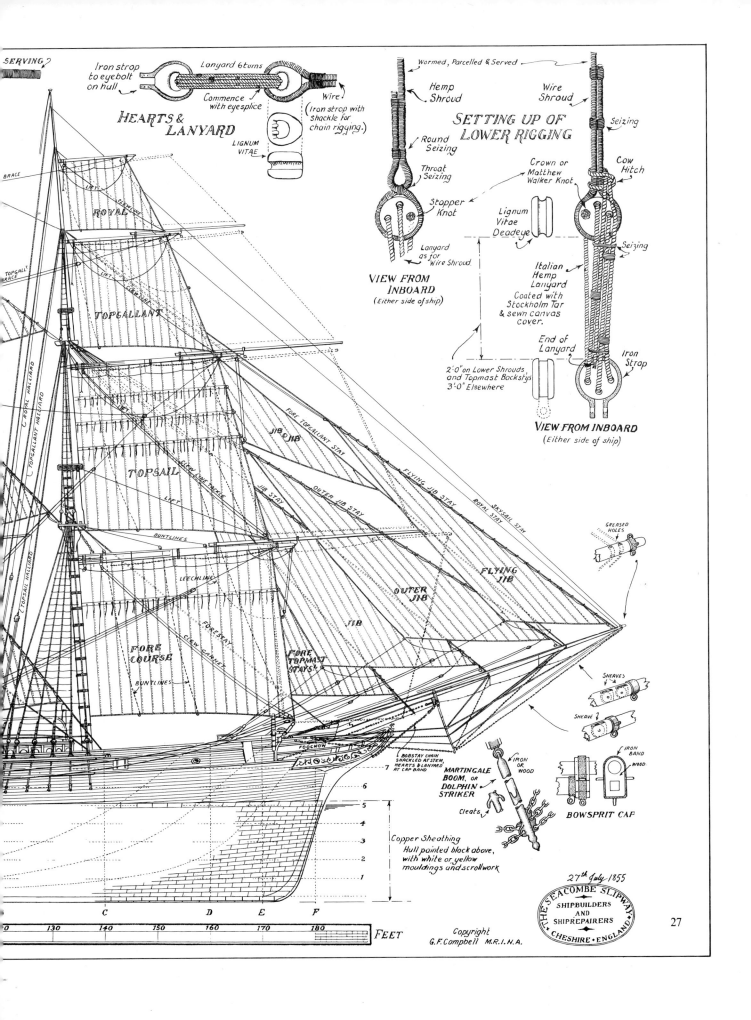

SERVING?

HEARTS & LANYARD

Iron strap to eyebolt on hull

Lanyard 6 turns

Commence with eyesplice

Wire (Iron strap with shackle for chain rigging.)

LIGNUM VITAE

SETTING UP OF LOWER RIGGING

Wormed, Parcelled & Served

Hemp Shroud

Wire Shroud

Round Seizing

Seizing

Throat Seizing

Crown or Matthew Walker Knot

Cow Hitch

Stopper Knot

Lignum Vitae Deadeye

Seizing

Lanyard as for Wire Shroud.

Italian Hemp Lanyard Coated with Stockholm Tar & sewn canvas cover.

VIEW FROM INBOARD
(Either side of ship)

End of Lanyard

Iron Strap

2'-0" on Lower Shrouds and Topmast Backstys 3'-0" Elsewhere

VIEW FROM INBOARD
(Either side of ship)

BRACE

ROYAL

TOPGALL BRACE

LIFT

CLEWLINE

TOPGALLANT

LIFT

CLEWLINE

ROYAL HALLIARD

TOPGALLANT HALLIARD

TOPSAIL

CLEW LINE PIECE

LIFT

TOPSAIL HALLIARD

BUNTLINES

LEECHLINE

FORE COURSE

BUNTLINES

CLEW GARNET

FORESTAY

FORE TOPGALLANT STAY

JIB O JIB

FLYING JIB STAY

SKYSAIL STAY

ROYAL STAY

JIB STAY

OUTER JIB STAY

FORE TOPMAST STAYS

FOGGNOW

JIB

OUTER JIB

FLYING JIB

GREASED HOLES

SHEAVES

SHEAVE?

Bobstay chain shackled at stem, Hearts & Lanyard at cap band

MARTINGALE BOOM, OR DOLPHIN STRIKER

IRON OR WOOD

Cleats

IRON BAND

WOOD.

BOWSPRIT CAP

Copper Sheathing
Hull painted black above, with white or yellow mouldings and scrollwork

7

6

5

4

3

2

1

C   D   E   F

0   130   140   150   160   170   180

Feet

27ᵗʰ July 1855

Copyright
G.F. Campbell M.R.I.N.A.

THE SEACOMBE SLIPWAY
SHIPBUILDERS AND SHIPREPAIRERS
CHESHIRE · ENGLAND

composite construction (24) it will be noticed that the bottom of the floor plate is a straight sloping line towards the keel and the garboard plank is extra thick with a slight hollow fairing into the bottom planking. Lloyds made this a requirement in their first composite rules of 1867, whereby the garboard strakes had to extend two-thirds of the depth of keel and take horizontal bolts through the keel as well as vertical ones through the keel plate, the planks themselves being of extra thickness. Prior to this, on composite hulls, many of the garboard strakes had been giving trouble as they were wrought nearly parallel to the bottom planking and met the side of the keel at an acute corner, not permitting good horizontal bolting, with consequent leakage in the keel rabbet. In some instances the garboard area was designed with a pronounced concave hollow which brought the garboard strake almost sideways on to the keel with a deep vertical rabbet. This gave good connections and a deeper keel at the same time, it being laid in two vertical members because of the depth of the rabbet. But it also meant that the lower edge of the floor plate and its frame had to be shaped hollow, which required more work and wastage of plating. So by increasing the size of the garboard plank and those adjacent to it, to conform to Lloyd's requirements, a reasonable hollow garboard could be designed if required without a hollow, or with very little, in the internal ironwork. The famous *Thermopylae* (1868) had this arrangement, and the *Cutty Sark* (1869) slightly less so. The latter ship's original design for the midship section did have a pronounced hollow to the floor plate and frame, but this was probably altered for economic reasons as well as to conform to Lloyd's.

The last of the true tea clippers was the *Lothair,* composite built in London in 1870, and two others of the same year were of iron, the *Blackadder* and the *Halloween,* also built in London. From then onwards the iron and steel clippers, which were not quite so fine-lined and had entered the Colonial trade back in the 1850s for emigrants and wool, were left to carry on the tradition. Some of the tea clippers that remained joined them on the run to Australia and New Zealand, where speed was not economically vital.

The plans given for the ship *Foochow* are intended to show a typical British wooden tea clipper with her arrangement and structure. Lest the reader should be inspired to trace the vessel's history I would hasten to add that it is an entirely fictional creation, no tea clipper with such a name having ever existed as far as I am aware. If a reader should be desirous of making a model tea clipper without the laborious and uncertain research work required for an actual ship, he could use these plans as a basis and make any changes he wishes, keeping them appropriate to the period.

Under full sail, heeling over slightly, and rising and falling easily through the seas, a clipper must have presented a magnificent sight from another passing ship. Many eye-witnesses have left us enthralling descriptions; how sometimes the gleaming copper would be exposed down to the turn of bilge in the trough of a sea, or the keel lifting clear from the forefoot to nearly one-third of the length.

The usual colour scheme—copper bottom, black topsides with a thin gold or yellow ribband at deck level terminating each end in flowing scrollwork—is still the most regal way to paint a ship. If we add a polished brass rail capping the bulwark from end to end, it gives perfection.

The occasional light green hull of some tea clippers although beautiful was not as impressive as the black. The thin white ribband just above the copper line which was painted on the *Cutty Sark* in her retirement days was not authentic for her or any other tea clipper, and was a detraction.

Black and white painted ports, inherited from the genuine gunports of East Indiamen, were carried on by the Blackwall frigates, the transatlantic packet ships, the iron clippers in the emigrant trade, and finally the big windjammers, but there does not seem to be any record of either British or American tea clippers having them, although it is possible that one or two of the early Americans were exceptional—perhaps the *Houqua*.

Figureheads as a rule were plain white possibly with the hem of a garment in gold leaf, or the hair in black. Some life-like colouring is occasionally mentioned for figures in human form, as also for an emblem such as a heraldic shield. American ships sometimes had a heraldic beast or bird which was covered with gold leaf, the eagle being popular, as on the *Challenge* where a large eagle spread its wings into the flaring hollow each side of the stemhead.

Masts and spars looked their best when varnished or oiled on the natural wood and blackened at the mast doublings, from the futtock shrouds attachments to the caps including the tops, and at each yardarm extremity. Made masts with iron hoops and vertical grooved recesses between them often had the grooves picked out in white, with the mast and bands in black or just the bands alone in black. This looked elegant too and was seen more often on American ships. In other schemes masts and spars were all white, pale pink, light buff or completely black. Paintings or models which show yardarms only (that is, the outer extremity) as white on a natural wood or black spar, are not authentic. This question was raised many years ago, when men who lived through the tea clipper era were still alive, and they denied ever seeing such a painting scheme, nor do any contemporary paintings or models show it.

Decks were oiled, varnished, or scrubbed and bleached almost white, according to the nature of the timber used. Margin planks around deck structures were commonly of teak even if the remainder of the deck was

Chapter Five

Appearance

of a softer and lighter coloured wood, and the caulked seams in the waist of the ship were black. The raised poop decks were, as often as money permitted, of teak or an oiled hardwood, and the deck seams in white putty, purely for appearance. The white seams also appeared frequently on the tops of deckhouses.

Insides of bulwarks were a decorative artist's dream. Rarely were they painted one colour throughout. The divisions made by the stanchions were panelled with painted borders or actual wood panels with mouldings like cabinetmakers' work, which could be unshipped and stowed away when at sea. Sometimes portable panels also had landscape scenes painted on them in each division; up to what standards we can't tell, but probably of the style seen on gypsy caravans or canal boats. Plainer painted panels on iron bulwarks as well as wooden ones were in pleasant pastel shades such as white with pale blue, green or pink, on a border about 6 in. wide, and inside this border a thin stencilled line with elaborated corners, geometrical or flower patterned, the centre of the panel having a stencilled motif such as a tudor rose or diamond. Above the main rail, if there was a topgallant bulwark or rail it too was panelled in horizontal rounded oblongs with wood mouldings and painted inner stencil lines as on the bulwarks. The decorative scheme could also be carried across the low bulkhead formed by a raised poop or a forecastle. The heavier American ships with their high, stout bulwarks topped by thick planks for the monkey rail clamps did not as often have the divisions formed by stanchions and in consequence ran plain bands of colour from end to end, white and buff for instance, but enhanced them by adding thick horizontal mouldings and flowered tracery, often cut out of the planks themselves. On both sides of the Atlantic the waterway planks (or gutters if metal) were painted a darker contrasting colour such as blue, green, grey or buff. One extraordinary and extravagant feature of the bulwarks was the amount of brasswork. The inside moulded edges of main rails were often capped with brass like a split tube, and the top exposed edge also brass capped, end to end in some instances. The vertical bulwark stanchions were faced with rounded brass or had chamfered corners and mouldings top and bottom. It was a poor ship that left them plain. Belaying pins could be brass, hardwood or iron.

Deckhouses of teak on British ships were panelled in their construction with solid vertical posts or styles between groups of panels, and frequently an ironwork framing inside. The teakwork was varnished bright originally as no self-respecting shipbuilder would paint over good class wood if it was easily accessible for maintenance. Later, with reduced crews, some of the panels might get painted white, as also the curved moulding on the edge of the roof, which also gave a pleasing appearance. Less expensive deckhouses were made of tongue and groove boarding, two thicknesses

ORNAMENTAL DECKWORK

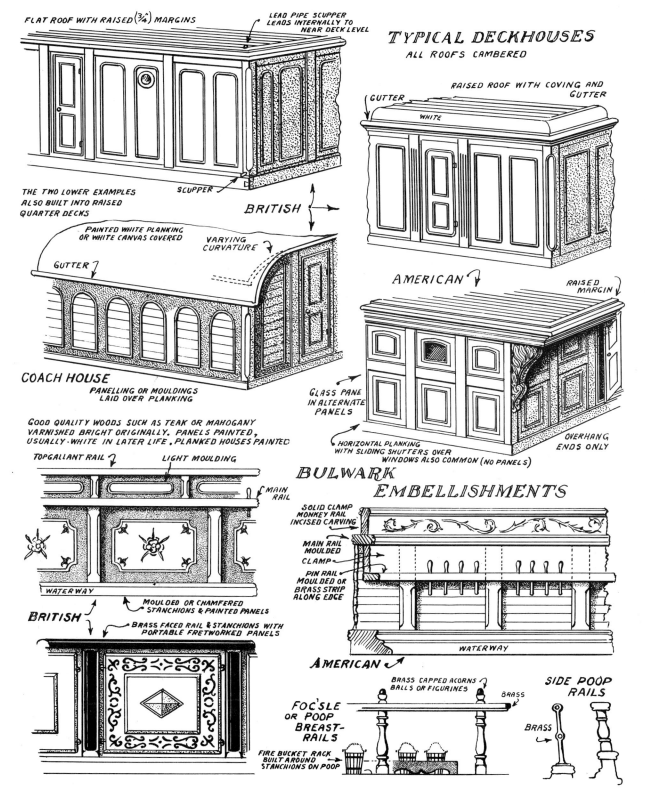

FLAT ROOF WITH RAISED (¾) MARGINS

LEAD PIPE SCUPPER LEADS INTERNALLY TO NEAR DECK LEVEL

TYPICAL DECKHOUSES
ALL ROOFS CAMBERED

RAISED ROOF WITH COVING AND GUTTER

GUTTER

WHITE

THE TWO LOWER EXAMPLES ALSO BUILT INTO RAISED QUARTER DECKS

SCUPPER

BRITISH

PAINTED WHITE PLANKING OR WHITE CANVAS COVERED

VARYING CURVATURE

GUTTER

COACH HOUSE

PANELLING OR MOULDINGS LAID OVER PLANKING

AMERICAN

RAISED MARGIN

GOOD QUALITY WOODS SUCH AS TEAK OR MAHOGANY VARNISHED BRIGHT ORIGINALLY. PANELS PAINTED, USUALLY WHITE IN LATER LIFE. PLANKED HOUSES PAINTED

GLASS PANE IN ALTERNATE PANELS

HORIZONTAL PLANKING WITH SLIDING SHUTTERS OVER WINDOWS ALSO COMMON (NO PANELS)

OVERHANG ENDS ONLY

TOPGALLANT RAIL

LIGHT MOULDING

MAIN RAIL

WATERWAY

BRITISH

MOULDED OR CHAMFERED STANCHIONS & PAINTED PANELS

BRASS FACED RAIL & STANCHIONS WITH PORTABLE FRETWORKED PANELS

BULWARK EMBELLISHMENTS

SOLID CLAMP MONKEY RAIL INCISED CARVING

MAIN RAIL MOULDED

CLAMP

PIN RAIL MOULDED OR BRASS STRIP ALONG EDGE

WATERWAY

AMERICAN

FOC'SLE OR POOP BREAST-RAILS

BRASS CAPPED ACORNS BALLS OR FIGURINES

BRASS

SIDE POOP RAILS

BRASS

FIRE BUCKET RACK BUILT AROUND STANCHIONS ON POOP

laid in opposite directions, the outer usually horizontal and painted overall white; American deckhouses were usually white.

Capstans in American ships were quite works of art according to some descriptions. Contrasting woods such as varnished mahogany and locust made up the main body, with brass whelps, and were topped with a polished brass dome together with composition metal rims for the handspikes and the base pawls. The British capstans, more often of iron, had the bright brass domed top but the remainder was painted black, white or green. Skylights and companionways were beautiful examples in teak or mahogany of the ship joiner's craft.

The mortices, tenons, dovetails, framing and panels were all thoughtfully designed to lock together for strength and durability against varying temperatures and salt water soakings. Hardwood gutters were let in under all opening joints, such that any water that entered was drained out again through miniature spouts. Items like these wheelboxes, vegetable lockers, flag and rope lockers, etc. were so well made that they outlived the ship even when neglected, and some survive today. I have seen them used as gardeners' lockers.

Apart from the panels, poop fronts could be found with elaborate carved figures as corbel supports under the deck overhang, and dolphins often decorated the cathead knee and the bulwarks at the hances where the levels changed. Even the butt ends of spare spars lashed to the deck or on the skids were painted with an emblematic star or diamond.

All this elaboration throws an interesting light on the personality of the men who owned and operated these craft. If the sole object in operating was the desire to make money, the ships would have been stripped down to bare necessities. Many of the owners were themselves retired mariners, or small personal syndicates not yet grown to the stature of the bigger, hard-headed, economy minded shipping companies. They were more like rich yacht owners, whose sole motivation was to own and sail a beautiful ship, and they were able to indulge in this pleasure by making her earn enough money, any extra profits being gladly acceptable. They had a concern as well, with few exceptions, for the men who joined them as crews in the adventure. The conditions for the seamen were good, when we consider the miserable housing from which many of them came in industrial England. The chief drawback was lack of adequate clothes-drying arrangements.

The true forecastle space in the bow was the poorest arrangement in British ships, as it sometimes, if on the upper level, accommodated the windlass and other gear as well. On the lower forepeak level this was avoided, but at the expense of space, being narrow and triangular and not too well ventilated.

American bow forecastles were larger and had more deck height, the

DECK FITTINGS

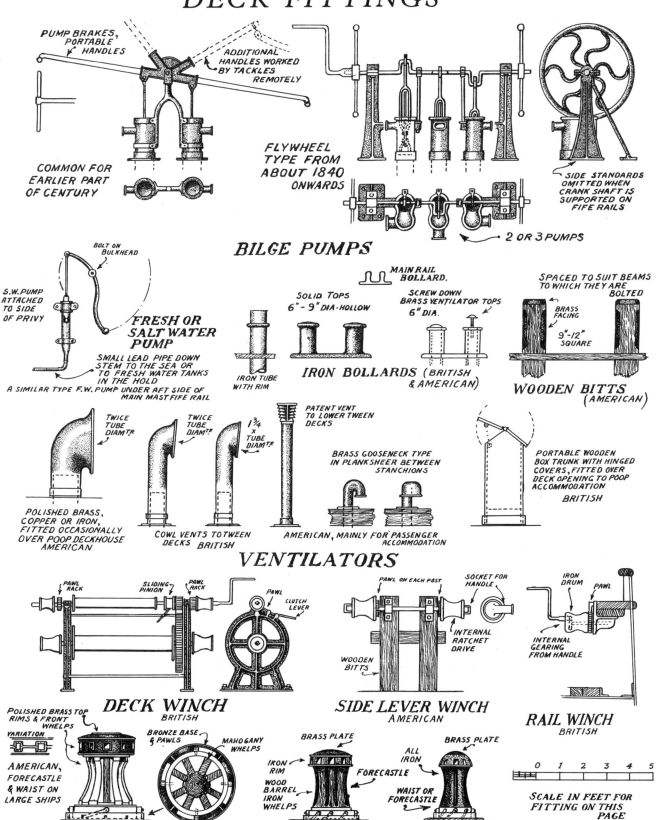

PUMP BRAKES, PORTABLE HANDLES

ADDITIONAL HANDLES WORKED BY TACKLES REMOTELY

COMMON FOR EARLIER PART OF CENTURY

FLYWHEEL TYPE FROM ABOUT 1840 ONWARDS

SIDE STANDARDS OMITTED WHEN CRANK SHAFT IS SUPPORTED ON FIFE RAILS

2 OR 3 PUMPS

BILGE PUMPS

BOLT ON BULKHEAD

S.W. PUMP ATTACHED TO SIDE OF PRIVY

FRESH OR SALT WATER PUMP

SMALL LEAD PIPE DOWN STEM TO THE SEA OR TO FRESH WATER TANKS IN THE HOLD

A SIMILAR TYPE F.W. PUMP UNDER AFT SIDE OF MAIN MAST FIFE RAIL

MAIN RAIL BOLLARD.

SOLID TOPS 6"-9" DIA-HOLLOW

SCREW DOWN BRASS VENTILATOR TOPS 6" DIA.

SPACED TO SUIT BEAMS TO WHICH THEY ARE BOLTED

BRASS FACING

9"-12" SQUARE

IRON TUBE WITH RIM

IRON BOLLARDS (BRITISH & AMERICAN)

WOODEN BITTS (AMERICAN)

TWICE TUBE DIAM.ᵀᴿ

TWICE TUBE DIAM.ᵀᴿ

$1\frac{3}{4}$ × TUBE DIAM.ᵀᴿ

PATENT VENT TO LOWER TWEEN DECKS

BRASS GOOSENECK TYPE IN PLANKSHEER BETWEEN STANCHIONS

PORTABLE WOODEN BOX TRUNK WITH HINGED COVERS, FITTED OVER DECK OPENING TO POOP ACCOMMODATION

BRITISH

POLISHED BRASS, COPPER OR IRON, FITTED OCCASIONALLY OVER POOP DECKHOUSE AMERICAN

COWL VENTS TO TWEEN DECKS BRITISH

AMERICAN, MAINLY FOR PASSENGER ACCOMMODATION

VENTILATORS

PAWL RACK

SLIDING PINION

PAWL RACK

PAWL

CLUTCH LEVER

PAWL ON EACH POST

SOCKET FOR HANDLE

IRON DRUM

PAWL

INTERNAL RATCHET DRIVE

WOODEN BITTS

INTERNAL GEARING FROM HANDLE

DECK WINCH
BRITISH

SIDE LEVER WINCH
AMERICAN

RAIL WINCH
BRITISH

POLISHED BRASS TOP RIMS & FRONT WHELPS VARIATION

AMERICAN, FORECASTLE & WAIST ON LARGE SHIPS

BRONZE BASE & PAWLS

MAHOGANY WHELPS

BRASS PLATE

IRON RIM

WOOD BARREL IRON WHELPS

FORECASTLE

ALL IRON

BRASS PLATE

WAIST OR FORECASTLE

0 1 2 3 4 5

SCALE IN FEET FOR FITTING ON THIS PAGE

CAPSTANS

upper deck level sometimes being set down to achieve this, but the deck-house in the waist (also called 'forecastle') which superseded that in the bow was healthier and lighter, although it was often flooded out in bad weather.

Furniture was of the sparsest. A plain scrubbed table pierced by two wooden posts up which it could slide and be pegged out of the way was the usual arrangement for messing, with long benches each side. Small tiered mess lockers were provided for each seaman for utensils, his clothing and personal effects being kept in his own chest. A small fresh water keg or tank was on hand inside the accommodation and a small iron stove, coal or wood fired, supplied the heating, the ship's coal supply being carried in a forepeak store. Lighting was given by gimballed oil lamps or sometimes shielded candles made of green tallow mixed with a rat poison.

Fresh water was pumped up from a large tank in the hold, one pump being on deck over the position of the tank, near the mainmast or poop, and another pump usually in the after saloon pantry. For washing and for toilets, etc. another small hand pump was fitted at the forecastle with a lead pipe leading forward and down the external stem to a point below the light waterline. It was let into the side of the stem and covered flush for protection, only a small hole being visible in the coppering.

Toilets for the crews were fitted in small wooden closets with curved or sloping roofs, touching the forecastle deck or a short distance aft of it. There could be two of these closets as toilets, one each side or sometimes with one of the pair used as a lamp room or locker. The toilet was flushed by hand from a can with salt water from the small pump adjacent. The larger iron or composite clippers with full height forecastles had the closets built in solid with the forecastle bulkhead.

Two similar closets were also built against the full height poop front bulkheads, for petty officers, in the larger ships, or again one compartment could be used as a storeroom. Additional toilet closets were fitted in the poop accommodation, with the captain's generally being private. These interior toilets often had a flushing tank filled by the steward or otherwise they too were flushed by hand.

Bathing was done with salt water on deck in a large flat wooden tub, when weather permitted, and this, with clothing purified with the fresh sea air, gave seamen that wonderful clean smell of the ocean which could be recognized ashore amidst its many odours. The wooden bunks with leeboards, in two tiers, varied in length in one compartment and were quite small by today's standards, being anything from 5 to 6 ft unless ample space permitted a uniform length. The men themselves were small and wiry, but possessed of great stamina from the simplest diet. I have the uniform and jacket of an East Indiaman's ship's surgeon of 1780 which would not fit my average sized son at the age of 11, his hand not passing further down the sleeve than the elbow, and the narrow sloping shoulders being about three-quarters the width of his. The smallness of men in the past often gives a misleading impression of the size of ships in contemporary prints where their heads barely appear over the bulwarks. Visitors to HMS *Victory* are often surprised at the smallness of the ship, having preconceived ideas of her size from paintings of battle scenes with numerous men occupying plenty of space.

A typical example of the stamina and courage of 19th century seamen is provided by the second voyage of the *Sir Lancelot* in 1866. Fitted with iron lower masts, she was leaving the Channel outward bound in December when she met with a heavy gale and increasing squalls. The bowsprit carried away first, followed by the foremast and mainmast near deck level, and in turn the mizzenmast above the top. This tremendous mess came hurtling down, tearing gaping holes in the deck and smashing bulwarks. The wreckage hanging over the side threatened to pound holes in the side of the hull, while the crew hacked away at the rigging and buckled iron masts, the foremast having snapped off at deck level. As many spars as possible were retrieved, and after Herculean efforts a jury mast was erected in the stump of the foremast; under jury rig the ship was manoeuvred back unaided to Falmouth in two days during the most vicious winter in fifty years. Six weeks later, with the help of expert riggers from Liverpool and new wooden lower masts sent down from London, the ship was repaired and on her way to China.

The after deckhouse, if there were two, would accommodate the ship's galley and probably two or more small cabins with double bunks for petty officers, cook, sailmaker, bosun or carpenter. The galley had an athwartships iron stove with storm rails, iron pan racks overhead, and coal and sand bins in the corners. The floor was usually laid with red quarry tiles or bricks, the living quarters having the wood deck itself covered with sailor-made rope mats. The windows in the earlier craft were glazed square openings with hinged or sliding wood shutters, followed in the 1850s by brass or iron framed circular portholes. The well known modern style of hinged brass portholes with rubber gaskets (originally cork) and large locking nuts appeared in the early 1860s. American ships kept the square shuttered type of window in the deckhouses later than the British, although they fitted circular metal framed fixed lights in the side hull or poop counter in the early 1850s. The old fashioned square stern sash windows persisted in some round-sterned British clippers in an artificial form, the sash and frame being raised wooden mouldings and the glass panes simulated in pale blue paint shaded in one corner for effect. The *Fiery Cross* (1855) had these.

British tea clippers, being built specifically for the tea trade, carried no more than two or three spare cabins for passengers or the owner in the

30 *Sir Lancelot* dismasted in the English Channel

MISCELLANEOUS FITTINGS

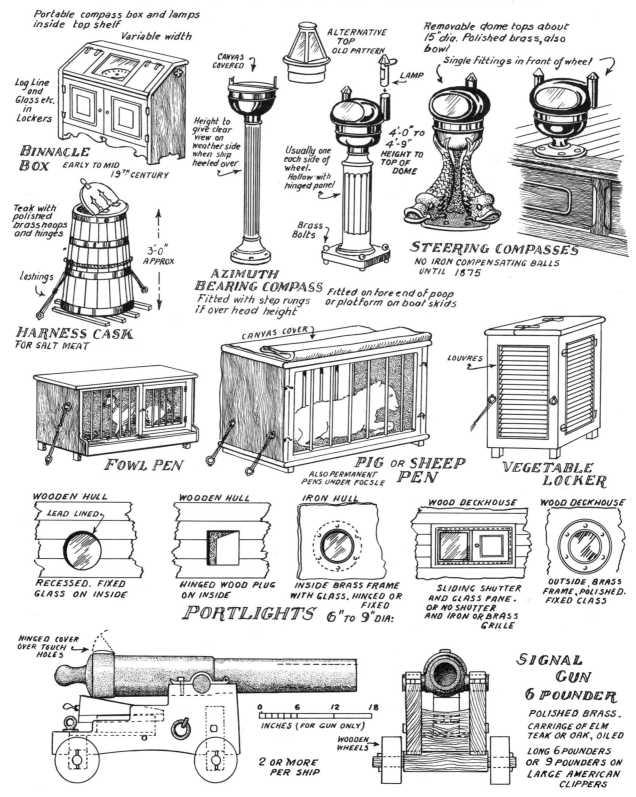

Portable compass box and lamps inside top shelf

Variable width

Log Line and Glass etc. in Lockers

BINNACLE BOX EARLY TO MID 19ᵀᴴ CENTURY

CANVAS COVERED

ALTERNATIVE TOP OLD PATTERN

LAMP

Height to give clear view on weather side when ship heeled over

Usually one each side of wheel. Hollow with hinged panel

Brass Bolts

Removable dome tops about 15" dia. Polished brass, also bowl

Single fittings in front of wheel

4'-0" to 4'-9" HEIGHT TO TOP OF DOME

STEERING COMPASSES
NO IRON COMPENSATING BALLS UNTIL 1875

Teak with polished brass hoops and hinges

Lashings

3'-0" APPROX

HARNESS CASK
FOR SALT MEAT

AZIMUTH BEARING COMPASS
Fitted with step rungs if over head height

Fitted on fore end of poop or platform on boat skids

CANVAS COVER

FOWL PEN

PIG OR SHEEP PEN
ALSO PERMANENT PENS UNDER FOCSLE

LOUVRES

VEGETABLE LOCKER

WOODEN HULL
LEAD LINED
RECESSED. FIXED GLASS ON INSIDE

WOODEN HULL
HINGED WOOD PLUG ON INSIDE

IRON HULL
INSIDE BRASS FRAME WITH GLASS, HINGED OR FIXED

WOOD DECKHOUSE
SLIDING SHUTTER AND GLASS PANE. OR NO SHUTTER AND IRON OR BRASS GRILLE

WOOD DECKHOUSE
OUTSIDE BRASS FRAME, POLISHED. FIXED GLASS

PORTLIGHTS 6" TO 9" DIA:

HINGED COVER OVER TOUCH HOLES

0 6 12 18
INCHES (FOR GUN ONLY)

2 OR MORE PER SHIP

WOODEN WHEELS

SIGNAL GUN 6 POUNDER

POLISHED BRASS. CARRIAGE OF ELM TEAK OR OAK, OILED

LONG 6 POUNDERS OR 9 POUNDERS ON LARGE AMERICAN CLIPPERS

poop accommodation. A typical layout of the poop house was a central saloon usually open to the aft end of the deck, with the spare cabins, pantry, captain's quarters and steward along the sides, and two or three cabins leading off alleyways for the mate (one berth), second and third officers (two berths) and perhaps apprentices. Other compartments would contain the medicine locker, pantry provisions, an armoury (a trunk around the rudder casing often stacked cutlasses or rifles) and sail locker. The low wings of a raised quarterdeck provided convenient storage for sails with a portable panel opening into the waist of the ship for easy removal. A flush deck hatch could be placed in the saloon floor leading to another storeroom in the afterpeak, dimly lit through a thick glass decklight from the saloon.

A ladderway from the saloon or alleyway opened onto the poop deck with a sliding top companionway forming a seat; and if it was a full height deckhouse, doors from the alleyway would open onto the upper deck as well. The usual choice for saloon and alleyway bulkheads was arched panelling, in mahogany, bird's eye maple or satinwood, with a darker wood for the fluted pilasters, skirtings etc. Cabin interiors were beaded tongue and groove boarding and painted, usually white, as also was the exposed wood deck overhead. Wooden beams might have chamfered or beaded corners, but steel or iron beams were always boxed in with mouldings and had open fret-work grilles between them for cabin ventilation along the lines of the bulkheads.

Most of these cabins had a horsehair sofa, a full height clothes locker, drawers under the bunk and sofa, and a metal washbowl in a stand covered by a hinged writing table flap. The captain had a larger bed than the normal bunk and a little more furniture, such as a bookcase, side-board, instrument cupboard, wardrobe and table in his own dayroom, and a small metal bath and toilet which might be fed from a hand-filled overhead tank. The saloon would have a small iron stove or miniature fireplace and a well made mahogany table with swivel chairs or padded bench with backrest. A piano was a favourite feature; and a sideboard cupboard with bevelled glass upper doors, mirror and shelves, well elaborated with carvings and brass rails, would contain culinary ware, wine glasses, bottles etc. All the furniture was always custom made to suit the sheer and camber at its position.

By contrast, American accommodation was the last word in luxury. Their clippers were not built specifically for the carriage of tea but for general cargo, and passengers who were accommodated in about a dozen state rooms in deckhouses or the long poop. The upper 'tween decks were also available for passengers. There are many descriptions in great detail of the clippers of the 1850s, the newspaper *Boston Atlas* having had a writer who gave eye-witness descriptions of some forty vessels

POOP ARRANGEMENTS

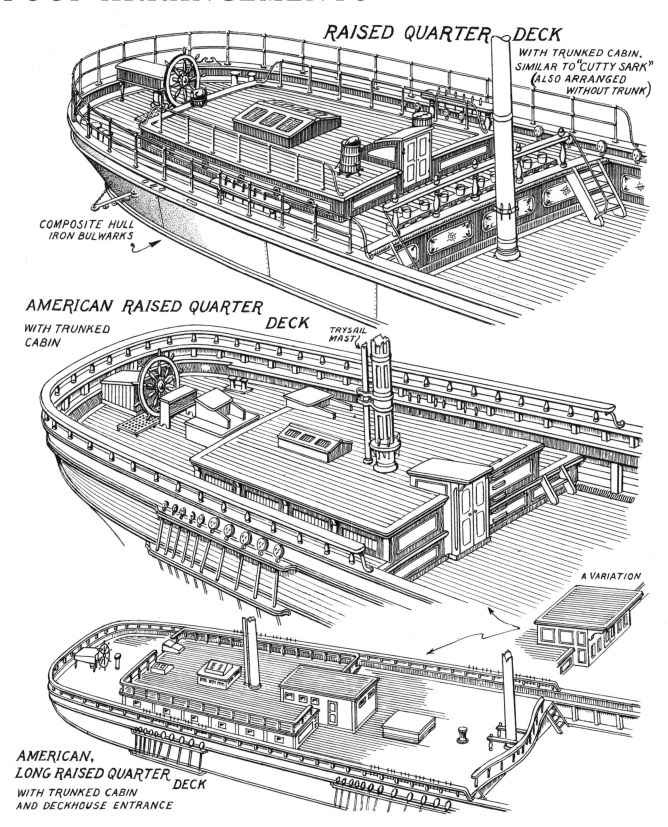

RAISED QUARTER DECK

WITH TRUNKED CABIN.
SIMILAR TO "CUTTY SARK"
(ALSO ARRANGED
WITHOUT TRUNK)

COMPOSITE HULL
IRON BULWARKS

AMERICAN RAISED QUARTER DECK

WITH TRUNKED
CABIN

TRYSAIL
MAST

A VARIATION

AMERICAN,
LONG RAISED QUARTER DECK

WITH TRUNKED CABIN
AND DECKHOUSE ENTRANCE

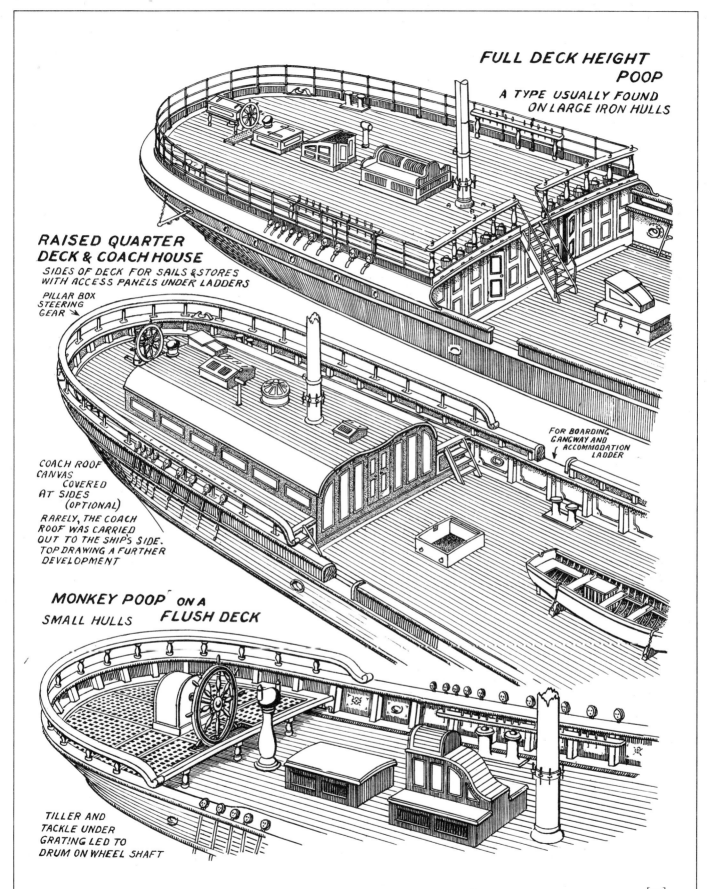

FULL DECK HEIGHT POOP
A TYPE USUALLY FOUND ON LARGE IRON HULLS

RAISED QUARTER DECK & COACH HOUSE

SIDES OF DECK FOR SAILS & STORES WITH ACCESS PANELS UNDER LADDERS

PILLAR BOX STEERING GEAR →

COACH ROOF CANVAS COVERED AT SIDES (OPTIONAL)

RARELY, THE COACH ROOF WAS CARRIED OUT TO THE SHIP'S SIDE. TOP DRAWING A FURTHER DEVELOPMENT

FOR BOARDING GANGWAY AND ACCOMMODATION LADDER

MONKEY POOP ON A FLUSH DECK
SMALL HULLS

TILLER AND TACKLE UNDER GRATING LED TO DRUM ON WHEEL SHAFT

[33]

from the Boston and New York vicinities as they were readied for their maiden voyages, and English writers also have left us accounts of some of them as they lay in the London docks.

Exotic contrasting woods were used in American ships for saloon and cabin panelling, or a white enamel finish with gilded mouldings and flowered ornamentation on the heads of fluted pilasters. Numerous framed mirrors and stained glass windows were also featured and there were more skylights to give light and air than on the British ships. The accommodation deck heights of 7 to 8 ft were higher than the British, which were under 7 ft, their deckhouses averaging 6 ft.

American deckhouses also favoured an overhanging deck edge on the fore side supported by long carved brackets. This was another indication of the relative dryness of American ships with their high freeboards, as such overhangs on British clippers would soon be damaged by seas.

The larger British sailing ships later in the century did have overhanging decks to the poop front, but they were not such wet ships as the clippers. Even so it was a dangerous form of design as a man could be lifted by a body of water and have his skull cracked under the overhang—which sometimes happened.

Externally the hulls on American clippers were frequently described as being glass smooth with an enamel-like finish. The seams of such planking would be finished off with a putty compound over the caulking. This would last until the ship started straining, when the seams would in-evitably show again. No doubt many British clippers had a similarly high quality finish also, but in some cases the adze was the finishing tool. The *Cutty Sark* when seen with light reflecting on the hull shows these adze marks quite distinctly, but possibly in her case the finishing touches were rather hasty, owing to financial troubles during her building.

The hull planking on wooden ships was thicker in the region of the waterline and some distance above it, this part being called the wales. In earlier times this thickened planking was made distinctly visible by a definite step down to the thinner planking both above and below it, and was usually painted black. Towards the period of the tea clippers the step was being eliminated by a gradual tapering down over three or four planks, at first on the lower side and then the upper, so that the whole hull had a smooth appearance. This was the case with the British clippers and some of the Americans. Other American clippers retained the upper step, sometimes with a moulding, which left a narrow strip of the hull between it and the planksheer, known as the waist. This area could occupy about six planks or less.

The bulwark planking was invariably thinner than the hull planking and consequently the top of the planksheer formed another step down, and as the planksheer projected, often as a special moulding, it formed

SOME TYPICAL DECK ARRANGEMENTS

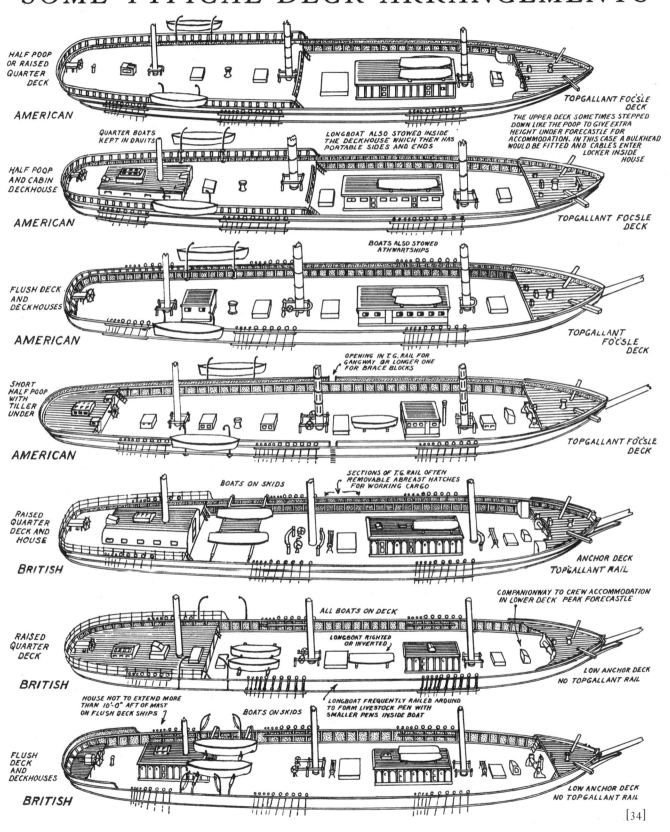

HALF POOP OR RAISED QUARTER DECK

AMERICAN

TOPGALLANT FOC'SLE DECK

THE UPPER DECK SOMETIMES STEPPED DOWN LIKE THE POOP TO GIVE EXTRA HEIGHT UNDER FORECASTLE FOR ACCOMMODATION. IN THIS CASE A BULKHEAD WOULD BE FITTED AND CABLES ENTER LOCKER INSIDE HOUSE

QUARTER BOATS KEPT IN DAVITS

LONGBOAT ALSO STOWED INSIDE THE DECKHOUSE WHICH THEN HAS PORTABLE SIDES AND ENDS

HALF POOP AND CABIN DECKHOUSE

AMERICAN

TOPGALLANT FOC'SLE DECK

BOATS ALSO STOWED ATHWARTSHIPS

FLUSH DECK AND DECKHOUSES

AMERICAN

TOPGALLANT FOC'SLE DECK

OPENING IN T.G. RAIL FOR GANGWAY OR LONGER ONE FOR BRACE BLOCKS

SHORT HALF POOP WITH TILLER UNDER

AMERICAN

TOPGALLANT FOC'SLE DECK

SECTIONS OF T.G. RAIL OFTEN REMOVABLE ABREAST HATCHES FOR WORKING CARGO

BOATS ON SKIDS

RAISED QUARTER DECK AND HOUSE

BRITISH

ANCHOR DECK TOPGALLANT RAIL

COMPANIONWAY TO CREW ACCOMMODATION IN LOWER DECK PEAK FORECASTLE

ALL BOATS ON DECK

LONGBOAT RIGHTED OR INVERTED

RAISED QUARTER DECK

BRITISH

LOW ANCHOR DECK NO TOPGALLANT RAIL

HOUSE NOT TO EXTEND MORE THAN 10'-0" AFT OF MAST ON FLUSH DECK SHIPS

BOATS ON SKIDS

LONGBOAT FREQUENTLY RAILED AROUND TO FORM LIVESTOCK PEN WITH SMALLER PENS INSIDE BOAT

FLUSH DECK AND DECKHOUSES

BRITISH

LOW ANCHOR DECK NO TOPGALLANT RAIL

quite a distinctive step. American clippers could therefore have as many as four mouldings on the hull if we include a main rail and monkey rail or topgallant rail.

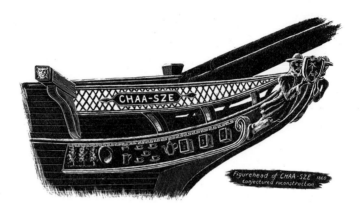

Figurehead of CHAA-SZE 1860
conjectured reconstruction

The era of the tea clippers saw important changes in the sail plans of ships. Early in the 19th century three-masted ships had each mast divided into three parts, the lower mast, the topmast and the topgallant mast. The mizzenmast before this time set a spanker, which was a development of the old triangular lateen with the portion before the mast omitted, and was loose footed with no boom. A boom was later fitted, but the mizzen lower yard or crossjack (cro'jack) was used only to spread the topsail, carrying no sail itself. The French called it *la vergue sèche*—the barren yard. It was not until the mid 1830s that an American skipper decided to set a sail on this yard, a move received with a little derision at first by his British counterparts as it was considered to have little effect, but by the next decade most American packet ships were carrying this sail, and eventually the British.

The topmasts carried only one sail, huge and difficult to handle, on the fore and main masts. It carried usually three rows of reef points, four on some of the largest American clippers. This single topsail had to be reefed or furled by men laying out on the yard, a task which could take up to half an hour.

In 1841 an American, Captain Forbes, devised a means of dividing this sail horizontally into two parts. The doubling of the lower and top masts was made longer than usual and an extra yard was added below the cap which could then be raised or lowered on its parral between the cap and the top. Above this the now shortened topsail was lowered to the cap as before. This was the origin of the double topsail, later to be followed by the double topgallant. Donald McKay fitted this arrangement on the famous *Great Republic*. This simple division of the sail was easier to work, and quicker, than the old single topsail as the upper topsail yard could be lowered from the deck and its sail then fell in front of the lower portion and was blanketed by it, the men then going aloft to furl it.

Another American shipmaster, Captain Howes, next brought out an improvement on this arrangement in 1853. In his version the new lower topsail yard was fixed to the lower mast cap with a movable crane and was additionally supported by an iron bar from the top. It would not move up or down however. The upper topsail on its still hoisting yard had its foot cut without any roach and was laced directly to the jackstay on the lower topsail yard without any gap, thus presenting an appearance as of a single topsail. The upper sail could be lowered quickly, thus saving the arduous task of reefing as with the single topsail, although it still had to be taken in and furled. This was but a step from the true double topsail first adopted in British clippers in 1865 with the *Ariel*, whereby the two sails were separate entities, with a slight gap between them.

In Howes' rig, when the upper portion was furled on its own yard, its foot was still laced to the lower yard. With the true double topsails how-

Chapter Six

Sail Plans

99

SAIL PLANS *of the* CLIPPERS

SINGLE OR PATENT REEFING TOPSAILS
SINGLE TOPGALLANTS, OPTIONAL ROYALS
SOMETIME BARQUE RIG WITH NO SQUARE
SAILS ON MIZZEN MAST

DOUBLE TOPSAILS ON FORE, MAIN AND MIZZEN
SINGLE TOPGALLANTS, ROYALS & SKYSAIL ON
  MAINMAST
MIZZENMAST OFTEN RETAINED SINGLE TOPSAIL

DOUBLE TOPSAILS
SINGLE TOPGALLANTS
ROYALS & SKYSAILS
MOONRAKERS OPTIONAL

DOUBLE TOPSAILS
DOUBLE TOPGALLANTS ON FORE & MAINMASTS
ROYALS (E.G. *Thermopylae*)

SPENCER ON FORE & MAINMAST
TRIANGULAR STAYSAILS ALSO FITTED ON ALL
STAYS INSTEAD OF OLD STYLE SAIL WITH NOCK
AS ABOVE AND IN PLACE OF THE SPENCERS

"JIMMIE GREEN" (UNDER JIBBOOM)
STUDDING SAILS ON FORE & MAIN MASTS
WATERSAILS OR FLYING KITES ON FORE & MAIN MASTS
RINGTAILS & WATERSAILS (END OF SPANKER)
MIZZEN TOPMAST STUDDING SAILS RARE

ever, the upper was furled completely on its own yard. Occasionally some captains still laced their upper topsails down as close as possible to the lower yards. The double topsails and double topgallants were the arrangement which persisted until modern times.

When a ship was fitted with single topsails and was lying in harbour with all sails furled, the lowered yards had a wide space between them, an appearance which their commanders took pride in. The upper yard of a double set, however, when lowered lay close in line with the lower one, an appearance which the old-timers hated. Therefore purely for appearance they would raise the upper yard with its furled sail to a position approximately halfway between the yards above and below, thus somewhat equalizing the spacing between all the yards as in the old style.

Aside from the developing double topsails, quite a number of ideas came out following on Howes' rig, all with the idea of making the large single topsail easier to handle. These were self-reefing sails on rolling spars, the best known being Cunningham's and Colling & Pinkney's, both British.

The general idea of Cunningham's invention was to reef and furl the single topsail on a revolving yard. The yard turned in two hoops at the yardarms which took the usual lifts and at the centre the mast parral also had a cogged sheave arrangement around which passed a chain tie. The two ends of the chain passed through sheaves at the topmast head and then down to the deck. By hauling on either one the yard could be made to rotate either way, being lowered or raised (parbuckling). The gear in the middle of the yard required the sail to be split into two halves down as far as the cap level, where a cross reef band was fitted. The gap was covered by a vertical strip of canvas (bonnet) which was laced to cross-battens at 12 in. intervals. The batten ends were grooved to fit around doubled rope bindings on each vertical edge of the sail. The bonnet could thus slide in the gap and bunch up like a Venetian blind. Battens tapered in an opposite direction to the yard taper enabled the sail to roll up on a parallel diameter. An additional spar about one-third the diameter of the yard was fitted parallel to it and just clear behind it, held by brackets from the yardarm hooks and at the middle sheaves. This spar did not revolve but took the footropes and stunsail booms, and could take the reef points for more security when the yard was lowered to the cap. The appearance of this sail when set was like a normal single topsail with a reef band at cap level and the vertical strip or bonnet looking like a ladder above it. It can be seen in the illustrations of the *Fiery Cross* (12) and *Lahloo* (13) and is often seen in old prints. The sail could only be close reefed, and to furl completely it needed men on the yard as usual.

Colling & Pinkney's differed chiefly in that the rolling spar to take the sail was not the actual yard but a lighter one supported in front of it by

DETAILS of TOPS

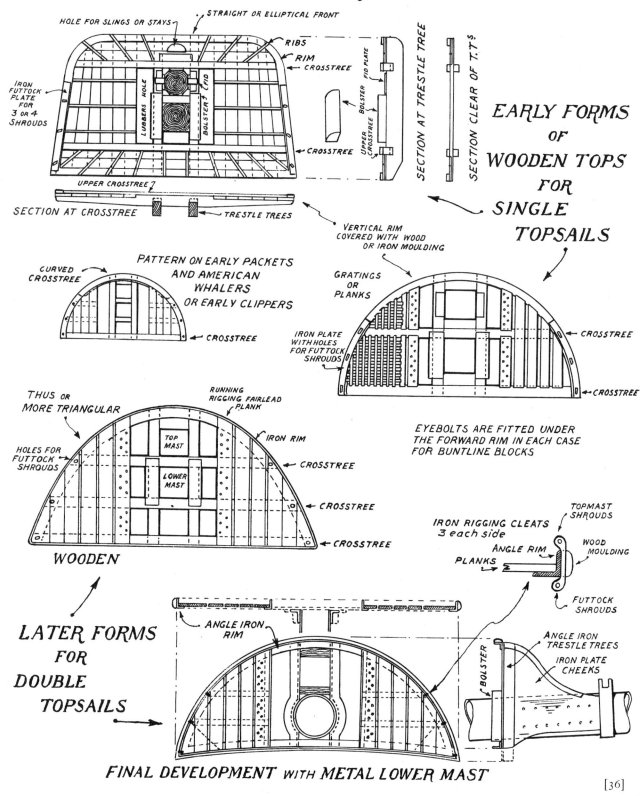

HOLE FOR SLINGS OR STAYS

STRAIGHT OR ELLIPTICAL FRONT

RIBS

RIM

CROSSTREE

FID PLATE

BOLSTER

UPPER CROSSTREE

CROSSTREE

IRON FUTTOCK PLATE FOR 3 OR 4 SHROUDS

LUBBERS HOLE

BOLSTER & FID

SECTION AT TRESTLE TREE

SECTION CLEAR OF T.T.s

UPPER CROSSTREE

SECTION AT CROSSTREE

TRESTLE TREES

EARLY FORMS OF WOODEN TOPS FOR SINGLE TOPSAILS

VERTICAL RIM COVERED WITH WOOD OR IRON MOULDING

CURVED CROSSTREE

PATTERN ON EARLY PACKETS AND AMERICAN WHALERS OR EARLY CLIPPERS

CROSSTREE

GRATINGS OR PLANKS

IRON PLATE WITH HOLES FOR FUTTOCK SHROUDS

CROSSTREE

CROSSTREE

EYEBOLTS ARE FITTED UNDER THE FORWARD RIM IN EACH CASE FOR BUNTLINE BLOCKS

THUS OR MORE TRIANGULAR

RUNNING RIGGING FAIRLEAD PLANK

IRON RIM

TOP MAST

LOWER MAST

CROSSTREE

CROSSTREE

CROSSTREE

HOLES FOR FUTTOCK SHROUDS

WOODEN

IRON RIGGING CLEATS 3 each side

ANGLE RIM

PLANKS

TOPMAST SHROUDS

WOOD MOULDING

FUTTOCK SHROUDS

LATER FORMS FOR DOUBLE TOPSAILS

ANGLE IRON RIM

BOLSTER

ANGLE IRON TRESTLE TREES

IRON PLATE CHEEKS

FINAL DEVELOPMENT WITH METAL LOWER MAST

yardarm attachments, the revolving action coming from a sheave arrangement at each end with chains up to the masthead working in a similar parbuckling action as Cunningham's. But the sail was intact without a split in the middle; also it could be furled completely on the yard by continued rotation.

Both these inventions were advantageous in that the reefing operation could be carried out from the deck by about two men, thus reducing the crew complement. They were in vogue for a short time, however, on clipper ships, being used latterly on the mizzen topsail only. Smaller vessels such as topsail schooners or brigs could be found with them well into the 20th century.

In the late 1860s the larger clippers fitted double topsails, but single topsails were more common.

The introduction of the double topsail also brought about a change in the shape of the tops on the lower mastheads, which the detail illustration explains (36). Originally tops with single topsails were very wide, about half the beam in warships to accommodate fighting men, less in merchant ships. They were either semicircular on the front rim or squarish, with the topmast shrouds attached to straight sides which gave them a good spread. There were two crosstrees to support the width, one on the aft side of the lower masthead and the other on the fore side of topmast heel, with a long narrow lubber's hole between. The wide spread of the foremost topmast shroud meant that when the topsail yard was braced at an angle, especially at half hoist in the reefed position, it would touch and chafe this shroud. By rounding the top into a semicircle to its after rim, this shroud was brought closer to the mast and thus allowed the yard to be braced without so much chafe. The forward crosstree now being so much shorter was moved between the two mast portions for better support of the top, and the long lubber hole was divided into two parts. Most American whalers and some packet ships in the first half of the century did not move this trestle tree, however, but compensated by strengthening the forward curved rim, a style that can be seen today in the whaler *Charles Morgan* (1841) at Mystic, Connecticut. However, once the double topsail was established with its lower yard always at a lower level, the foremost topmast shroud had to be brought in closer still, and this was achieved by making the top more triangular in shape with a rounded front, and on wooden tops usually with three crosstrees.

The advent of the metal lower mast brought about a metal rimmed top with plate cheek supports and no crosstrees. It was shorter in the fore and aft length and the sides were more angulated and on a gradual curve around the front rim in a pattern continued up to modern times.

The change in arrangement of the crosstrees followed somewhat the same principle as did the tops. From a framework with two wide crosstrees

DETAILS *of* TOPMAST CROSSTREES

EARLY PATTERN OF WOODEN CROSSTREES FOR WOODEN MASTS

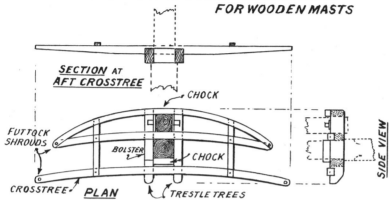

SECTION AT AFT CROSSTREE

CHOCK

FUTTOCK SHROUDS

BOLSTER

CHOCK

CROSSTREE · PLAN

TRESTLE TREES

SIDE VIEW

THE INNER SURFACES OF THE APERTURE FOR THE TOPMAST HEEL HAVE NAILED FILLING PIECES TO MAKE UP FOR THE SMALLER MAST, THE TRESTLE TREES BEING EQUIDISTANT THROUGHOUT

TOPGALLANT SHROUDS REEVE THRO' THE HOLES IN THE ENDS OF WOODEN CROSSTREES, OR ACROSS THE FORK IN THE IRON CROSSTREES, AND THENCE SET UP TO A FUTTOCK BAND SHACKLE BELOW WITH LANYARDS. LATTERLY THE FUTTOCK SHROUDS WERE IRON RODS WITH EYES AT THE TOP TO TAKE SMALL DEADEYES OR BULLSEYES FOR LANYARDS. BACKSTAYS RAN FREE IN EARLIER SHIPS, AND LATER IN THE CLEATS ON THE SPREADERS, BEING LEATHERED AND OFTEN SEIZED IN PLACE

LATER PATTERN OF WOODEN CROSSTREES

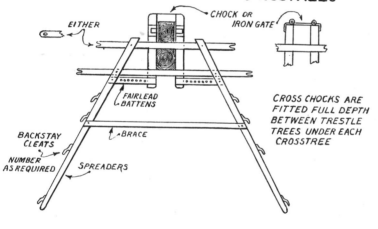

EITHER

CHOCK OR IRON GATE

FAIRLEAD BATTENS

BACKSTAY CLEATS

BRACE

NUMBER AS REQUIRED

SPREADERS

CROSS CHOCKS ARE FITTED FULL DEPTH BETWEEN TRESTLE TREES UNDER EACH CROSSTREE

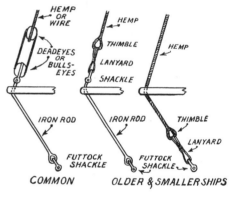

HEMP OR WIRE

DEADEYES OR BULLS-EYES

IRON ROD

FUTTOCK SHACKLE

COMMON

HEMP

THIMBLE

LANYARD

SHACKLE

IRON ROD

FUTTOCK SHACKLE

HEMP

THIMBLE

LANYARD

OLDER & SMALLER SHIPS

ARRANGEMENTS OF FUTTOCK SHROUDS

CROSSTREES FOR IRON TOPMASTS & WOODEN TOPGALLANT MASTS

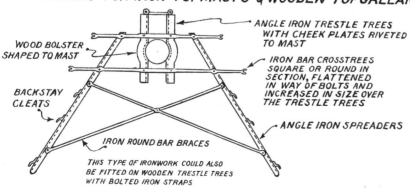

WOOD BOLSTER SHAPED TO MAST

BACKSTAY CLEATS

ANGLE IRON TRESTLE TREES WITH CHEEK PLATES RIVETED TO MAST

IRON BAR CROSSTREES SQUARE OR ROUND IN SECTION, FLATTENED IN WAY OF BOLTS AND INCREASED IN SIZE OVER THE TRESTLE TREES

ANGLE IRON SPREADERS

IRON ROUND BAR BRACES

THIS TYPE OF IRONWORK COULD ALSO BE FITTED ON WOODEN TRESTLE TREES WITH BOLTED IRON STRAPS of near equal length they became shorter as described above, the foremost in particular in order for the shroud to clear the braced yard. Also the ever-increasing height of mastheads required very long backstays to the top-gallant, royal and skysail hounds, of such a length that they could not easily be kept taut without undue strain. To increase their effective angles, spreaders were angled outwards from across the crosstrees to touch each backstay in line, and hold them a little further out by means of cleats. They were usually held in these cleats by seizings or locking pins. Spreaders did not become common until the second half of the century, however. They were stiffened by cross-bracings either straight across or diagonally, which had to clear braces from mizzen, topgallant and royal yards which sometimes led to the main topmast trestle trees.

The running rigging of American ships was often envied by British seamen because it was lighter to handle and had larger blocks, which also by mid-century were fitted with patent roller-bushed sheaves. One reason for this increased size of blocks was that American running rigging was made of manila, which was slightly weaker than the hemp used on British ships and therefore had to be increased in size for an equivalent breaking strain. Apart from this, however, the blocks were made larger for easier working, according to comments made by earlier writers, a fact which did not convince British shipowners who preferred smaller and neater looking blocks aloft.

Hemp was used for standing rigging on American ships, however, long after it had been superseded by wire on the British vessels.

Chapter Seven

Sails

One of the more obvious ways of distinguishing American merchant ships at sea during the 19th century, as against the British or European, was the colour of the sails. The Americans used heavy cotton duck, which stood out snowy white in the distance, whereas the British used flax canvas sometimes with a hemp mixture, which appeared as a greyish or pale fawn colour, which although likely to become bleached in time, never had the same snowy whiteness as cotton. American naval ships often carried flax canvas. Centuries before, the lowest sails of the old galleon types were made of a coarse heavy material known as kersey, and some contemporary references name these sails as kerses, which may possibly be the origin of the word course or coarse, although the word course in other contexts also means a layer or row, such as in bricks or slates. Ships usually carried a spare suit of sails, and the oldest worn canvas, well patched, would be used in fair weather regions, changing to the best canvas for heavy weather.

The sail cloths were assembled by sewing overlapping seams, the best method known as double round seam. The perimeter of the sail was folded over (tabled) about 4 to 6 in. for the lower courses, 3 to 5 in. for topsails, and 3 in. for smaller sails, and to this hem was stitched a stout bolt-rope always on the after side of square sails and not the extreme edge. Additional strength was given by sewing an extra cloth of canvas (lining) over the side edges (leeches); a folded cloth horizontally at the reef points; a narrower one at the foot (roach) and a short distance up; and one at the head, with vertical cloths part way up the sail in line with each buntline, all of these except at the head being on the fore side of the sail.

The seams were an average of $1\frac{1}{2}$ in. wide, but on fore and aft sails varied somewhat. The spanker seams were wider at the foot, say 3 to $3\frac{1}{2}$ in. occasionally 5 in., and about $2\frac{3}{4}$ in. at the head, in the main body being $1\frac{1}{2}$ in. Each seam tapered gradually to these widths, which helped to make up the shape of the non-parallel sides and gave a slight convex curve (roach) at the foot and slight bag in the middle. Occasionally American spankers were made from extra wide duck of 42 in. width of bolts, but a false seam was stitched in the middle to preserve the stiffness and flatness. Large jibs had seams about 3 in. at the foot and $2\frac{1}{2}$ in. along the stay. Some sailmakers, carrying on with an old tradition, gave belly to the square sails also, but the most efficient sails were made as flat as possible, Americans excelling at this, with the cotton duck often looking like 'veneered boards covered with white beads'.

The success of the famous yacht *America* in 1851 has been attributed to this. An interesting account is recorded by a steamship officer on seeing the *America* approaching off the Isle of Wight apparently without any mainsail set. 'So completely was the sail covered [hidden] by the mainmast that not a particle of it was visible; there was no belly to the sail and the gaff

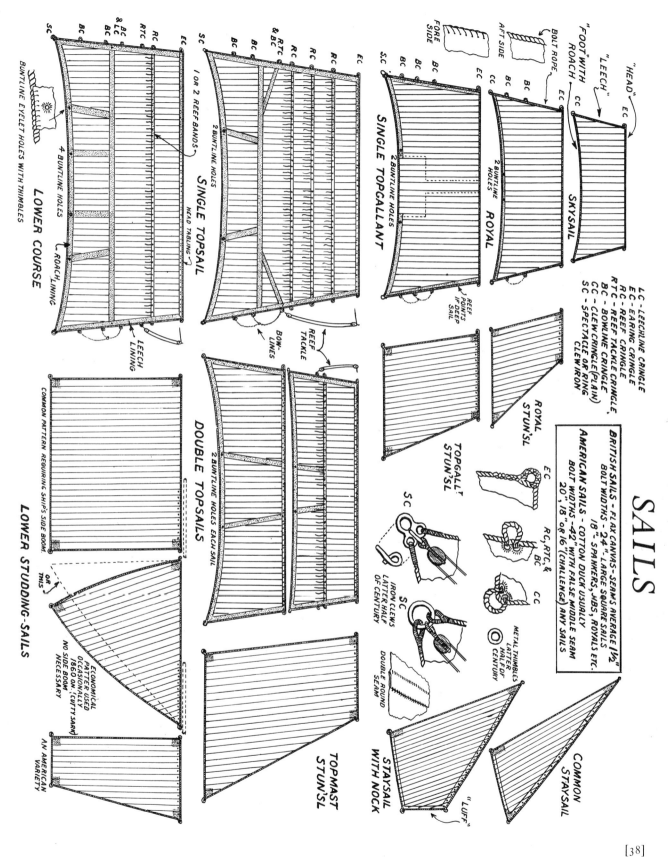

SAILS

BRITISH SAILS - FLAX CANVAS - SEAMS AVERAGE 1½"
BOLT WIDTHS - 24". LARGE SQUARE SAILS
18". SPANKERS, JIBS, ROYALS ETC.
AMERICAN SAILS - COTTON DUCK USUALLY
BOLT WIDTHS -42" WITH FALSE MIDDLE SEAM
20", 18" OR 16" (CHALLENGE) ANY SAILS

L.C - LEECHLINE CRINGLE
E.C - EARING CRINGLE
R.C - REEF CRINGLE
R.T.C - REEF TACKLE CRINGLE
B.C - BOWLINE CRINGLE
C.C - CLEW CRINGLE (PLAIN)
S.C - SPECTACLE OR RING
CLEW IRON

"HEAD"

"LEECH"

"FOOT" WITH ROACH

FORE SIDE

AFT SIDE

BOLT ROPE

SKYSAIL

ROYAL

2 BUNTLINE HOLES

SINGLE TOPGALLANT

REEF POINTS IF DEEP SAIL

ROYAL STUN'SL

TOPGALL' STUN'SL

SINGLE TOPSAIL

HEAD TABLING

1 OR 2 REEF BANDS

2 BUNTLINE HOLES

REEF TACKLE

BOW- LINES

LOWER COURSE

BUNTLINE EYELET HOLES WITH THIMBLES

4 BUNTLINE HOLES

ROACH LINING

LEECH LINING

E.C

R.C, R.T.C & B.C

C.C

S.C IRON CLEWS LATER HALF OF CENTURY

S.C DOUBLE ROUND SEAM

METAL THIMBLES LATTER HALF OF CENTURY

DOUBLE TOPSAILS

2 BUNTLINE HOLES EACH SAIL

COMMON PATTERN REQUIRING SHIP'S SIDE BOOM

LOWER STUDDING-SAILS

ECONOMICAL PATTERN USED OCCASIONALLY 1860 ON (CUTTY SARK) NO SIDE BOOM NECESSARY

OR THIS

AN AMERICAN VARIETY

TOPMAST STUN'SL

STAYSAIL WITH NOCK

"LUFF"

COMMON STAYSAIL

[38]

was exactly parallel to the boom.' This sail was also laced to the boom, an innovation to British designers, and was said to be soaped or greased also. Lacing would only be applicable on ships to a spanker with lowering gaff, and not until the 1860s did it appear on a British ship. It was reserved more for schooners and seldom seen on clipper types.

The illustrations show the method of working in the attachments of rigging etc. to the boltropes. Early in the century the cringles were formed of rope only, but later they had metal cringles inserted. With rope cringles for the buntlines along the foot, the sail had a tabling only, but when the buntlines were fastened in holes in the edge of the sail itself, a lining was added to the tabling.

The position of the reef points is of interest to the artist. From the previous century the holes through which the reef points were threaded were pierced in the cloth between the seams, sometimes in pairs and sometimes alternating two and one per cloth, as also were the holes for lacing to the jackstay. Often a middle line of stitches was sewn down a seam, especially on naval craft, and the reef band cloth being doubled over was probably considered strong enough to take the reef points clear of the seams. Contemporary paintings and some photographs over the latter half of the century show the reef points as being on the line of the seam more often than not, and some windjammer photographs late in the century plainly show reef points spaced seam and cloth alternately.

Spankers seem to be consistent throughout the century in having their reef points on the seam lines, possibly because these seams were wider and the stitched holes helped to keep them tighter. It was a complaint that wide seams held water and caused rot.

The spacing of the holes for the hanks in staysails was 36 in. for the lighter ones such as flying jibs, the larger ones being 27 in., which may or may not have coincided with the seams, depending on the angle of the seams relative to the luff.

The curved roach on a square sail was dependent on the angle or height of the stay immediately below it, which it had to clear. Braces from the yards on a mast in front sometimes led downward under the sail, attaching either to the mast or the head of the stay, and these also had to be cleared. The roach of the upper of the double topsails was the least, and in some cases it was straight and laced to the lower topsail yard. British clippers tended to keep the leeches of the courses almost vertical and the leeches of the sails above in a good taper to a small skysail or royal, while some of the best American ships ran all the leeches in a straight tapering line from the clew of the courses up to the skysails, truly a 'pyramid of sail'.

The clews of square sails and fore and aft sails for merchant ships early in the century were made as separate rope cringles sewn to the corners of the boltrope (naval sailmakers made the clew by working a loop in the boltrope itself). These clews frequently broke and metal thimbles were fitted in them for extra strength, and by about mid-century solid metal iron clews were used, either in ring form or as a fashioned spectacle iron, either of which would outlive the sail. The bowline cringles, which once were fitted on all ships' square sails, survived on a few clippers to the end of the era. They had a useful function in holding the windward leech of the sail well forward and in a slight curve to catch the wind in the body, as without them the tack, on the courses, or sheet on upper sails, pulled the leech into a straight line. Bowlines went out of fashion mainly because they were extra tackle to maintain and operate.

The shape of the lower studdingsails (stunsails) depended largely on the width of the lower course itself, which if very wide in spread would need a narrower stunsail. A boom extended this stunsail outboard and was fitted to a gooseneck from the ship's side abreast the mast which would be on the rim of the channels if there were any. This boom could be about 55 ft long and 12 in. in diameter, but shorter ones were more practicable. It could be eliminated by making the stunsail triangular to meet the ship's side as was done in the case of the *Cutty Sark*, although many modern paintings of her wrongly show a boom with a rectangular stunsail. Stunsails were fitted each side of the mast on the fore and main, and on rare occasions on the mizzen topsail. With the wind from aft both sides would be set abaft their adjacent sails, but with the yards braced a small amount the stunsails on the lee side would be set on the fore side of their adjacent sails, until the yards were braced sharply when the lee ones would be taken in.

They were stowed vertically with lashings to the insides of the topmast shrouds, when frequently required; otherwise on the boat skids or deck-house roof. The lower stunsail booms were housed along the side of the fore channel on each side, resting in a crutch about a third of its length from the end.

Another form of boom resembling the lower stunsail boom and mentioned at times for some tea clippers was called the passaree boom. This was a shorter boom fitted each side of the foremast from a gooseneck at a height to clear the bulwark. Each boom was set athwartships, their lengths extending slightly beyond the foreyard. With a following wind and the sail set square athwartships, each clew would be extended from these booms thus making the sail lie nearly flat. Without them the clews would be held in close to the bulwarks with the sail forming a rounded belly as was the case with the main course. The booms could be stowed from their goosenecks to crutches on the forecastle deck or removed entirely.

The workmanship and design of sails was of the greatest importance and if badly done could largely nullify the performance of an otherwise well designed ship. Wrinkles around the boltropes, seams or linings were

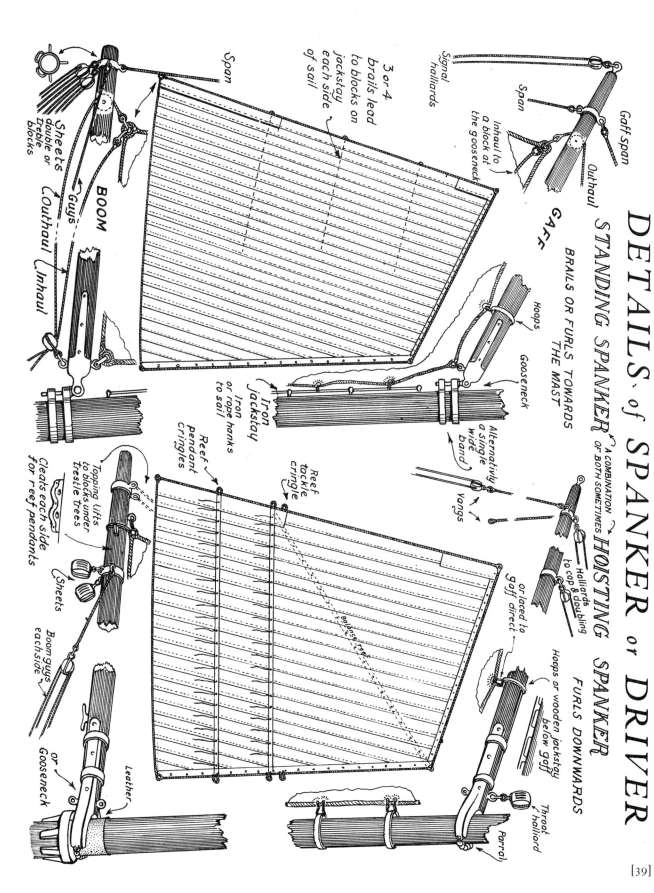

DETAILS of SPANKER or DRIVER

STANDING SPANKER
A COMBINATION OF BOTH SOMETIMES

HOISTING SPANKER

BRAILS OR FURLS TOWARDS THE MAST

FURLS DOWNWARDS

Gaff span

Span

Span

Outhaul

Signal halliards

Inhaul to a block at the gooseneck

3 or 4 brails lead to blocks on jackstay each side of sail

GAFF

Sheets double or treble blocks

Outhaul

Inhaul

Guys

BOOM

Hoops

Gooseneck

Iron jackstay or rope hanks to sail

Alternativly a single wide band

vangs

Halliards to cap & doubling

Hoops or wooden jackstay below gaff

Throat halliard

Reef pendant cringles

Reef tackle cringle

or laced to gaff direct

Topping lifts to blocks under trestle trees

Cleats each side for reef pendants

Sheets

Boom guys each side

or Gooseneck

Leather

Parral

[39]

usually a sign of poor workmanship with uneven tensions between the cloth of the sail and its various stitchings and ropings.

Chapter Eight

Masts and Spars

Wherever possible wooden lower masts were made from a single tree which was first squared down to the maximum square possible and then into the round, leaving only the head and possibly the heel square. The mizzen mast, being relatively small, was usually a single tree. Its smooth surface was also convenient for the hoops of the spanker sail to ride up and down on, as also the gaff jaws if so rigged.

If the fore and main masts could not be taken out of a single tree, owing to their size, it was necessary to build up each mast to its required diameter by joining or splicing a number of smaller timbers longitudinally. The minimum number was known as a five-piece mast, which meant that a central spindle was made out of one piece in a square taper extending for part of the upper length, and then each face built up with separate lengths, rounded on their outer surface and long enough to make up the full required length, as shown.

The central spindle extended above the level of the trestle trees to form the masthead, with two of the side pieces reduced in size to strengthen it. To provide rigidity to the whole mast it was necessary to prevent the longitudinal abutting surfaces from sliding against each other, which would happen if the whole mast was allowed to bend. To stop this, each of these surfaces was carved out (tabled) in alternating raised lips and sunken mortices (coaks) which interlocked when bound tightly together. The binding was done by iron hoops put on hot while they were in an expanded condition, shrinking tight when cooled. A very large mast could be made up by this process, using as many as fourteen pieces for the whole. In the five-piece mast the side pieces were known as 'side trees' and the fore and aft pieces respectively as 'fore side fish' and 'after side fish'.

British ships' masts made this way, with five or more pieces, had the appearance of a plain round mast hooped at regular intervals, the hoops usually distinctively painted black or white (yellow in the Royal Navy after Trafalgar). Many of the American masts elaborated the process by not making up a full circular section. Instead the edges of the outer pieces were chamfered off, leaving four vee-shaped grooves running up the mast, and in order to make a solid bed on which to tighten up the iron bands a small wedge piece was fitted in each groove under the band. The ends of these wedge pieces were sloped to prevent water lodging against them. The idea of the grooves was to eliminate feather edges on the side timbers and allow air circulation nearer the heart of the mast, thus reducing the possibility of rot, which is always a danger when timbers are buried inside other timbers.

These grooved masts looked quite handsome, especially when the grooves were picked out in a different colour, say black or white, or some-times red. Some of the masts on the steamship *Great Britain* were made in

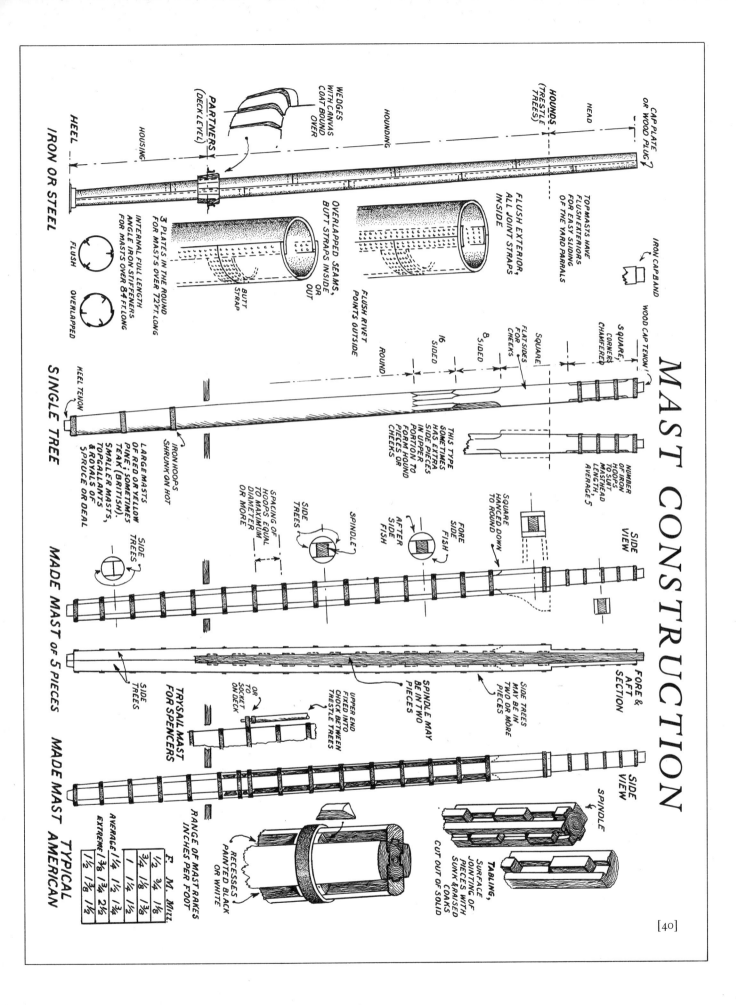

MAST CONSTRUCTION

[40]

this manner, and possibly on some sailing vessels too, but usually it was an American characteristic.

If spencers or trysails (the small fore and aft sails with gaff, on the fore or main masts) were fitted on large hooped masts, the mast would be too large to conveniently take the gaff jaws or the hoops on the luff of the sail, so a much smaller mast was stepped close to the larger with its head let into a chock between the trestle trees and its foot stepped in a socket on deck or to a mast band with an eye or socket a foot or so above the deck. This small diameter mast took the gaff jaws and also the wooden hoops seized to the sail. If the mizzenmast was considered too large it also would have a trysail mast, which served the same purpose as the extra mast which distinguishes a small craft called a snow. A vertical iron rod jackstay bolted to the aft side of the mast with a gooseneck fitting on a band for a hooked iron on the end of the gaff, served the same purpose as the trysail mast and by mid-century seems to have been fairly common on wooden masts and was carried on in the same fashion for iron masts. The gaff of course was the non-lowering type, and the head of the trysail ran on hoops along it with an outhaul and inhaul, the body of the sail being brailed from blocks attached to the jackstay or mast.

Iron masts were built intermittently from early in the century, especially for steamships, but it was in the 1860s, with the composite clippers, when they became the general rule, at first for lower masts only and then for topmasts as well. The lower yards and bowsprit were also of iron, and the lower topsail yards, if large enough. The extra strength of iron masts coupled with the more rigid iron wire rigging encouraged a greater spread to the courses which was apparent in the later clippers.

Iron masts, however, had their problems too, and many collapsed, chiefly due to localized bad riveting and insufficient internal stiffening. The restricted space inside the masts made it difficult for rivets to be held up efficiently while being hammered on the outside, and if a small man or boy could not do it, a long rod was used as a lever to hold up a heavy iron dolly like a long mallet fitting against the rivet head, which was inserted from the inside.

I recall an incident during the reconstruction of the *Cutty Sark* involving one of these dollies, with near-fatal results. One of the ship's masts, which had been a replacement after a dismasting, was found to be some feet too short, and in consequence I suggested adding the requisite length to the heel, thus avoiding altering the top and its cheek plates. This meant raising the mast by chain hoists inside the hold, seized around a heavy iron bar which passed through two holes burned out of the mast. The mast had a full-length vertical diaphragm plate as a stiffener, and a manhole was cut into the mast near the holes so that the diaphragm could be penetrated also. After the strain had been taken on the hoists, a shipwright put his

MASTHEADS

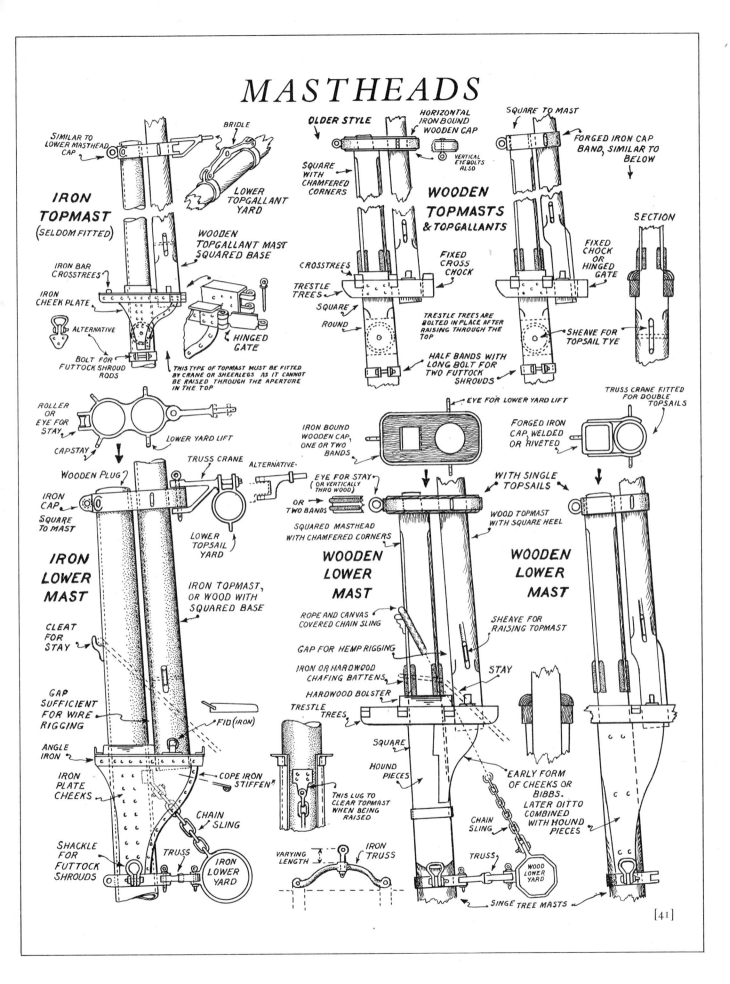

IRON TOPMAST (SELDOM FITTED)

SIMILAR TO LOWER MASTHEAD CAP

BRIDLE

LOWER TOPGALLANT YARD

WOODEN TOPGALLANT MAST SQUARED BASE

IRON BAR CROSSTREES

IRON CHEEK PLATE

ALTERNATIVE

HINGED GATE

BOLT FOR FUTTOCK SHROUD RODS

THIS TYPE OF TOPMAST MUST BE FITTED BY CRANE OR SHEERLEGS AS IT CANNOT BE RAISED THROUGH THE APERTURE IN THE TOP

WOODEN TOPMASTS & TOPGALLANTS

OLDER STYLE

HORIZONTAL IRON BOUND WOODEN CAP

VERTICAL EYEBOLTS ALSO

SQUARE WITH CHAMFERED CORNERS

CROSSTREES

TRESTLE TREES

SQUARE

ROUND

FIXED CROSS CHOCK

TRESTLE TREES ARE BOLTED IN PLACE AFTER RAISING THROUGH THE TOP

HALF BANDS WITH LONG BOLT FOR TWO FUTTOCK SHROUDS

SQUARE TO MAST

FORGED IRON CAP BAND, SIMILAR TO BELOW

FIXED CHOCK OR HINGED GATE

SHEAVE FOR TOPSAIL TYE

SECTION

ROLLER OR EYE FOR STAY

CAPSTAY

LOWER YARD LIFT

WOODEN PLUG

IRON CAP

SQUARE TO MAST

IRON LOWER MAST

CLEAT FOR STAY

GAP SUFFICIENT FOR WIRE RIGGING

ANGLE IRON

IRON PLATE CHEEKS

SHACKLE FOR FUTTOCK SHROUDS

TRUSS

TRUSS CRANE

LOWER TOPSAIL YARD

ALTERNATIVE

IRON TOPMAST, OR WOOD WITH SQUARED BASE

FID (IRON)

COPE IRON STIFFEN?

CHAIN SLING

IRON LOWER YARD

VARYING LENGTH

THIS LUG TO CLEAR TOPMAST WHEN BEING RAISED

IRON TRUSS

IRON BOUND WOODEN CAP, ONE OR TWO BANDS

EYE FOR LOWER YARD LIFT

EYE FOR STAY (OR VERTICALLY THRO WOOD)

OR TWO BANDS

SQUARED MASTHEAD WITH CHAMFERED CORNERS

WOODEN LOWER MAST

ROPE AND CANVAS COVERED CHAIN SLING

GAP FOR HEMP RIGGING

IRON OR HARDWOOD CHAFING BATTENS

HARDWOOD BOLSTER

TRESTLE TREES

SQUARE

HOUND PIECES

CHAIN SLING

TRUSS

WOOD LOWER YARD

SINGE TREE MASTS

TRUSS CRANE FITTED FOR DOUBLE TOPSAILS

FORGED IRON CAP, WELDED OR RIVETED

WITH SINGLE TOPSAILS

WOOD TOPMAST WITH SQUARE HEEL

WOODEN LOWER MAST

SHEAVE FOR RAISING TOPMAST

STAY

EARLY FORM OF CHEEKS OR BIBBS. LATER DITTO COMBINED WITH HOUND PIECES

[41]

42 Barque *Strathmore* in Canning Drydock, Liverpool, 1857

head into the manhole to see if all was correct and as he withdrew it, a loud clatter was heard as a heavy iron dolly came hurtling downwards and bounced upwards again from the keel. It must have jammed inside near the masthead during construction and suddenly loosened with the vibration.

Another method of stiffening up a metal mast was to fit internal angle bars for the full length, and doubling plates at deck level, but nevertheless when made in ill-equipped shipyards such masts frequently failed. The smithwork, such as capbands and trusses, also varied from being neat and well formed to crudely fabricated pieces hammer-welded together, which logbooks frequently reported as giving way.

In general appearance, the single tree wooden mast and the iron mast had a taper from the deck to the hounds, and built masts had very slight taper, if any at all.

Topmasts with a few exceptions were more commonly of wood, and topgallants which also incorporated royal masts were of wood, tapering down in the round to the truck. The transition from the topgallant to royal mast was made with a very slight shoulder which stepped down in diameter, over which a thick rope grommet was placed, this serving as a stopper for the rigging (stays, etc.) to prevent it sliding down the mast. Another way was to fit a copper cylinder or funnel above the shoulder with a slight projecting flange on its lower rim. The spliced eyes of the back-stays, the topgallant shrouds' seized eyes, and fore and aft stays were all fitted snugly on this funnel. Its purpose was to retain all this rigging in place whenever the topgallant mast was lowered down, so that when the shoulder position passed through the cap band all the stays, etc. hung slack from the funnel, which would then be resting on the cap. On raising the mast again, the funnel would catch on the step and hoist to its original position with the rigging taut again.

The reason for lowering the topgallant masts was that tea clippers in dock with a minimum of ballast were very often temporarily unstable, and on a number of occasions actually heeled over onto dockside sheds, as did the *Cutty Sark* once in London. Therefore as much top weight as possible was lowered when a clipper ship was in dock with an empty hold. The jib-boom was also usually withdrawn on entering dock, but this was to prevent it fouling other ships, or poking into someone's bedroom in adjacent terraced houses.

The peaks of the masts on British ships were crowned with flat wooden trucks, like flattened buns, which contained two small sheaves for flag halliards. American trucks were distinguished by a spherical ball, usually gilded. The tallest mast would or should have had a lightning conductor also.

Wooden yards were made out of single trees, except some of the largest lower yards in American ships, which were made of two pieces spliced or fished together with coaks, as for the mast, and bound with iron hoops. The large spars were first cut down with adzes to the square, from the natural tree shape. The required taper to the yardarm was then marked off, and the square shape reduced to an octagonal for about the middle quarter length. Outside this length the spar was then shaped to a tapering round, the taper having a slight curve. The smallest spars might be left round in the centre section if the natural tree happened to be the right size. The eight-sided middle portion of the larger yards could also have the corners taken off again for sixteen sides, except that the after side flat was left large if it had to take a wooden yoke. No doubt, in some instances the yard was rounded off over the middle portion to avoid special smithwork on the iron bands, but it was more usual to leave eight or sixteen sides.

Iron yards for the lower topsail and possibly upper topsail yards were round, tapered, riveted tubes with open ends into which wooden plug yardarms were fitted.

The outer stunsail boom iron in its most common arrangement had two long straps bolted through the yardarm with the hoop set upwards and forwards at about 45°. There were some exceptions to this whereby the stunsail booms were slung below the yard and slightly aft of its centre to clear the chain sheets which ran below the yard. The *Cutty Sark, Spindrift, Lord of the Isles, Glenaros, Fiery Cross* of 1860, and *Great Republic* were rigged in this manner. The outer boom iron could also be detachable with its bent arm having a square prong which fitted into a square hole in the end of the yard, or else have a square hoop on the end of the iron to fit over a square iron on the yardarm tip with a locking pin.

The jackstay bar to which the sail was attached was, on most of the clippers, an iron rod which went through a series of eyebolts either spiked into a wooden yard or riveted onto an iron one. There was a separate rod for each side, placed slightly forward of the central axis and held in place by forelock pins through the rods at each of their ends. Prior to this, earlier in the century, jackstays had been made either of wooden battens with a series of long apertures on the underside between the bolts or nails, or else a hemp or wire rope on each side leading through eyebolts and tightened in the centre by a connecting lanyard.

The fitting below the centre of the lower yards to lead the topsail chain sheets down to the deck was, during the 1860s, in the form of two iron sheaves each with a separate pin, with cheek plates and straps, called a bullock block (43). Instead of this single fitting two separate iron blocks, each attached to its own iron yard band, could be fitted, being an older arrangement from the times when sheets were of hemp instead of chain.

For the yards which were not fixed in one position by a truss or crane —see the mastheads drawing (41)—a chain tye was attached to the central

DETAILS of TIMBER and IRON YARDS

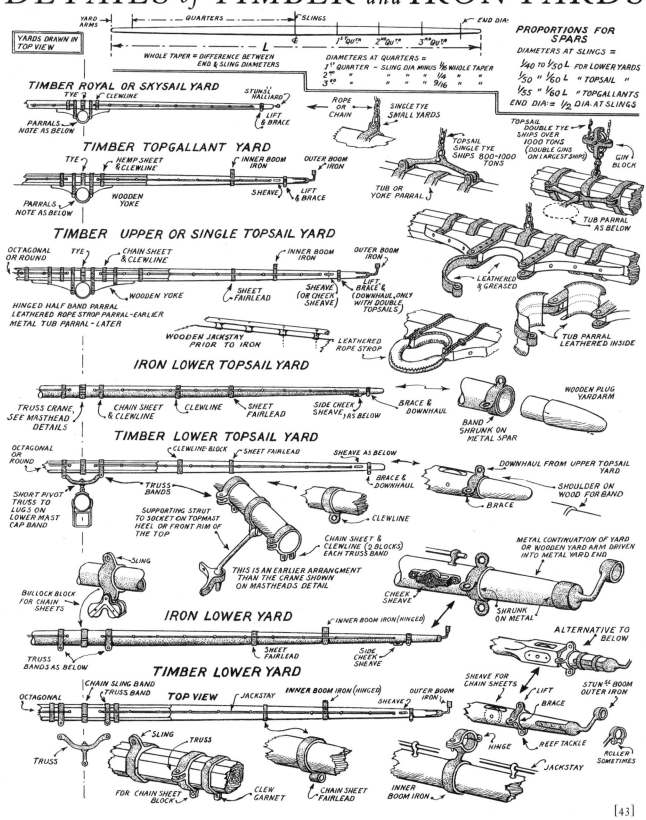

YARDS DRAWN IN TOP VIEW

YARD ARMS — QUARTERS — SLINGS — END DIA.

L

WHOLE TAPER = DIFFERENCE BETWEEN END & SLING DIAMETERS

DIAMETERS AT QUARTERS =
1ST QUARTER - SLING DIA MINUS 1/16 WHOLE TAPER
2ND " " " " 1/4 "
3RD " " " " 9/16 "

PROPORTIONS FOR SPARS
DIAMETERS AT SLINGS =
1/40 TO 1/50 L FOR LOWER YARDS
1/50 " 1/60 L " TOPSAIL "
1/55 " 1/60 L " TOPGALLANTS
END DIA. = 1/2 DIA. AT SLINGS

TIMBER ROYAL OR SKYSAIL YARD
TYE — CLEWLINE — STUNS'L HALLIARD — LIFT & BRACE
PARRALS NOTE AS BELOW

ROPE OR CHAIN — SINGLE TYE SMALL YARDS

TIMBER TOPGALLANT YARD
TYE — HEMP SHEET & CLEWLINE — INNER BOOM IRON — OUTER BOOM IRON
PARRALS NOTE AS BELOW — WOODEN YOKE — SHEAVE — LIFT & BRACE

TOPSAIL SINGLE TYE SHIPS 800-1000 TONS

TOPSAIL DOUBLE TYE SHIPS OVER 1000 TONS (DOUBLE GINS ON LARGEST SHIPS) — GIN BLOCK

TUB OR YOKE PARRAL

TUB PARRAL AS BELOW

TIMBER UPPER OR SINGLE TOPSAIL YARD
OCTAGONAL OR ROUND — TYE — CHAIN SHEET & CLEWLINE — INNER BOOM IRON — OUTER BOOM IRON
WOODEN YOKE — SHEET FAIRLEAD — SHEAVE (OR CHEEK SHEAVE) — LIFT, BRACE & (DOWNHAUL, ONLY WITH DOUBLE TOPSAILS)

HINGED HALF BAND PARRAL
LEATHERED ROPE STROP PARRAL - EARLIER
METAL TUB PARRAL - LATER

LEATHERED & GREASED

WOODEN JACKSTAY PRIOR TO IRON — LEATHERED ROPE STROP

TUB PARRAL LEATHERED INSIDE

IRON LOWER TOPSAIL YARD
TRUSS CRANE, SEE MASTHEAD DETAILS — CHAIN SHEET & CLEWLINE — CLEWLINE — SHEET FAIRLEAD — SIDE CHEEK SHEAVE, AS BELOW — BRACE & DOWNHAUL

BAND SHRUNK ON METAL SPAR — WOODEN PLUG YARDARM

TIMBER LOWER TOPSAIL YARD
OCTAGONAL OR ROUND — CLEWLINE BLOCK — SHEET FAIRLEAD — SHEAVE AS BELOW
SHORT PIVOT TRUSS TO LUGS ON LOWER MAST CAP BAND
TRUSS BANDS — BRACE & DOWNHAUL
SUPPORTING STRUT TO SOCKET ON TOPMAST HEEL OR FRONT RIM OF THE TOP
CHAIN SHEET & CLEWLINE (2 BLOCKS) EACH TRUSS BAND
THIS IS AN EARLIER ARRANGEMENT THAN THE CRANE SHOWN ON MASTHEADS DETAIL

DOWNHAUL FROM UPPER TOPSAIL YARD — SHOULDER ON WOOD FOR BAND — BRACE — CLEWLINE

METAL CONTINUATION OF YARD OR WOODEN YARD ARM DRIVEN INTO METAL YARD END
CHEEK SHEAVE — SHRUNK ON METAL

SLING
BULLOCK BLOCK FOR CHAIN SHEETS

IRON LOWER YARD
TRUSS BANDS AS BELOW — INNER BOOM IRON (HINGED) — SHEET FAIRLEAD — SIDE CHEEK SHEAVE

ALTERNATIVE TO BELOW

SHEAVE FOR CHAIN SHEETS — LIFT — STUNS'L BOOM OUTER IRON
BRACE — HINGE — REEF TACKLE — ROLLER SOMETIMES — JACKSTAY

TIMBER LOWER YARD
OCTAGONAL — CHAIN SLING BAND — TRUSS BAND — TOP VIEW — JACKSTAY — INNER BOOM IRON (HINGED) — OUTER BOOM IRON — SHEAVE

TRUSS — SLING — TRUSS — FOR CHAIN SHEET BLOCK — CLEW GARNET — CHAIN SHEET FAIRLEAD — INNER BOOM IRON

[43]

band or to an iron span, depending on its size. The single chain tye led up through a sheave in the mast and then down to the bulwarks with a rope purchase, this part being known as the halliard. The large American clippers with their heavy wooden topsail yards had a double chain tye from the yard, made fast to a trestle tree, led down to an iron gin block on the yard, back up again to another gin block on the other trestle tree and then down to the bulwark with a halliard purchase. This could be varied by doubling the arrangement, with two gin blocks on the yard and the lead going to the opposite hand, or else leaving a single gin block on the yard and a gin block under each trestle, whereby there was a purchase from each side of the ship, either of which could hoist or lower the yard independently.

Of the various parral arrangements on the drawing (43), that with the leathered metal tub was most common on the later tea clippers, and survived into the end of the sailing ship period. This arrangement did not normally apply to very small yards for which the yoke arrangement was used with a simple rope parral.

As a spare mast or spar, a large spar known as the hermaphrodite spar was lashed down with chains to eyebolts on the deck either close to the waterway or alongside the hatch coamings. This spar, square in section with the corners chamfered, was of a size that could be converted either to a topmast or a lower yard. In addition there was a spare topsail yard either on deck alongside the hermaphrodite spar or along the top of the forward deckhouse reaching towards the forecastle. This was the minimum required on a ship over 600 tons, and instead of the hermaphrodite spar separate spars of lengths to suit the topmast and lower yards could be carried, together with as many other minor spars as the owner desired. Most of these would be carried on top of a deckhouse on raised beams or skids, and small light spars across the after boat skids between the boats. The masts for the boats themselves would also be carried here, together with stunsail booms. The skid beams would have two pillar supports each, if carrying such weight.

Chapter Nine

Coppering

The original purpose of sheathing the underbody of a ship was to protect it against the teredo shipworm which in tropical waters could infest a wooden hull and in a short time eat its way inside the wood sufficiently to sink the ship. This pest eventually found a home in European waters having been brought there in infected hulls. The cheapest protection was a layer of wood sheathing about 2 in. thick laid over the hull planking with various mixes in between such as tar or tallow mixed with hair, sulphur or ground glass. East Indiamen used to pay their bottoms with a mix of oil, dammar resin and blacking when careened out east, before the days of coppering. It was also desirable to reduce the growth of seaweed and barnacles on the hull, and various metals were originally tried such as lead or zinc, and in some instances leather. The metals were unsuccessful, in salt water at least, because electrolytic action was set up between dissimilar metals such as the iron fastenings in the hull and iron gudgeons etc. against the sheathing metal and its fastenings. One method that persisted for a time was to stud the wood sheathing with large-headed cast iron nails as close together as possible, this however being only to resist shipworm.

Finally after much experimentation the use of copper plates with copper nails to fasten them was accepted about 1783, the hull fastenings, gudgeons, pintles etc. being of copper or copper alloys such as bronze. In cases where the copper was to be put on a hull with iron fastenings, wooden sheathing had to be used as an insulator, although the gudgeons and pintles had to be of bronze.

The copper sheets were originally nearly pure copper which eroded away quickly even though it kept a good clean bottom, the marine growth being shed along with the eroding copper. This was an expensive process and efforts were made to reduce the rate of erosion, or exfoliation, by adding other metals. Muntz introduced a mixture of 50 parts copper to 50 parts zinc in 1830, and by 1846 had changed it to 60 of copper and 40 of zinc, which was the well known Muntz metal in use up to modern times, sometimes with a proportion of tin added. Lloyd's Registers of the period describe ships' bottoms as being yellow metalled, coppered or brass bottomed, all these being slight variations. It was still a very expensive method of dealing with a ship's hull, from the labour point of view as well as material cost. Figures for an East Indiaman's construction give the cost of coppering at one-tenth the cost of the hull. A ship could expect to get two Far East voyages before needing recoppering. The notorious Confederate raider *Alabama* left Laird's yard in England in July 1862. By December 1863 Captain Semmes reported her copper as largely destroyed, a factor which contributed to her defeat by the *Kearsarge* in June 1864, by which time the remaining copper was hanging in long ribbons. The famous American clippers *Oriental* of 1849 and the *Challenge*

COPPERING

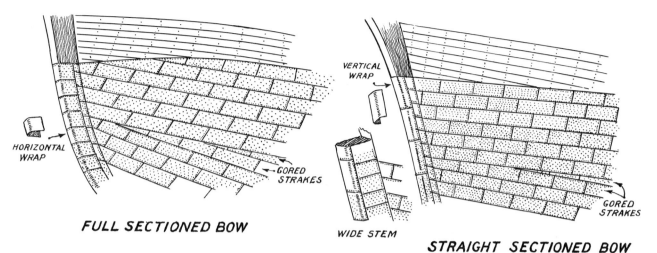

FULL SECTIONED BOW

HORIZONTAL WRAP

GORED STRAKES

VERTICAL WRAP

WIDE STEM

STRAIGHT SECTIONED BOW

GORED STRAKES

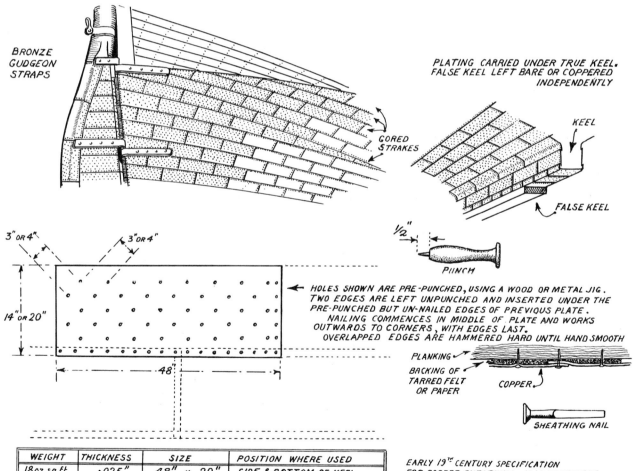

BRONZE GUDGEON STRAPS

GORED STRAKES

PLATING CARRIED UNDER TRUE KEEL. FALSE KEEL LEFT BARE OR COPPERED INDEPENDENTLY

KEEL

FALSE KEEL

$\frac{1}{2}"$

PUNCH

3" OR 4"

3" OR 4"

14" OR 20"

48"

HOLES SHOWN ARE PRE-PUNCHED, USING A WOOD OR METAL JIG. TWO EDGES ARE LEFT UN-PUNCHED AND INSERTED UNDER THE PRE-PUNCHED BUT UN-NAILED EDGES OF PREVIOUS PLATE. NAILING COMMENCES IN MIDDLE OF PLATE AND WORKS OUTWARDS TO CORNERS, WITH EDGES LAST. OVERLAPPED EDGES ARE HAMMERED HARD UNTIL HAND SMOOTH

PLANKING

BACKING OF TARRED FELT OR PAPER

COPPER

SHEATHING NAIL

WEIGHT	THICKNESS	SIZE	POSITION WHERE USED
18 oz sq.ft	·025"	48" × 20"	SIDE & BOTTOM OF KEEL
28 " "	·038"	48" × 14"	BOTTOM, BILGE & SIDE
32	·044"	48" × 14"	BOWS & WIND-WATERLINE AREA

EARLY 19TH CENTURY SPECIFICATION FOR COPPER SHEATHING - H.M. DOCKYARDS. SIZES MAINTAINED THROUGHOUT THE CENTURY FOR LARGE SHIPS AND SUITABLE FOR MERCHANTMN of 1851 had to be drydocked for recoppering fifteen months after their launch. The main trouble was that the mixture for the copper alloy was not consistent throughout, owing to imperfect manufacturing methods, and the sheathing nails themselves could be different, which meant that the deterioration of the plates was piecemeal, a condition which was aggravated progressively as the plates were renewed piecemeal also. Another cause of plate deterioration on fully wooden hulls was puckering, and the loosening of nails due to the twisting movement of the hull when riding diagonally across heavy seas. Such movement could be considerable, opening up seams on the weather side and compressing them on the lee side.

The copper plates could be nailed directly to the planking over a tar or pitch coating, or in the best work over tarred paper or felt about $\frac{1}{4}$ in. thick. After nailing, the plates were hammered down along the exposed edges until hand smooth. The nails sometimes were hammered so that they gave a quilted effect to the sheathing, but this was considered bad practice. The varying sizes of plates and their relative positions are given in drawing (44) which shows naval and merchant ship practice. Very small craft would use smaller plates.

Although the ideal system of laying the plates was to have the exposed edges of the butts facing aft, and those of the seams on the lower edge, this arrangement helping to keep a loose plate reasonably flat by gravity and water flow, it was only achieved on very small craft where probably a single gang of workmen would work progressively in one direction, as a modelmaker would plate a model. However with a large ship in drydock or on the slip this would take too long, and several gangs would be working together, some from amidships towards the bow or stern and some from the waterline downwards or keel upwards. This would mean that the exposed edge of the seams and butts would vary in their relative positions on different parts of the hull, which can sometimes be seen on contemporary photographs.

With multiple gangs the shipwright would have to mark off the run of the plates carefully. The areas where gored strakes were necessary would be useful for meeting points. The standard rectangular plates were cut as little as possible, which meant that on certain hull forms the uppermost strake was not always continuous or parallel from stem to sternpost. If the top edges of the uppermost strake were necessarily cut to form the waterline the discarded pieces would be used as far as possible to form the gores elsewhere. The waterline for the coppering was not a true horizontal but had a gentle sheer to it, as was done with all waterlines, whether painted or coppered. It would be approximately 18 in. above the load waterline aft to 30 in. forward and drop to 12 in. amidships, on a large clipper.

The appearance of the copper, varying slightly with the composition from reddish to yellowish, would be like an old copper coin, when it was freshly applied. At sea in salt water it would be bright and shiny, and in port or drydock a light green when dry, like a copper dome.

An eye-witness in the mid-19th century gives a most thrilling description of a naval squadron under full sail in the Channel, majestically rising and dipping in the swell with the wet copper glinting and flashing in the setting sunshine.

Chapter Ten

Steering Gear Arrangements

The form of steering gear with a vertical spoked wheel introduced early in the 18th century worked a long wooden tiller below decks on the fore side of the rudder post, from a revolving wooden drum or barrel with hide ropes and a system of pulleys. The system was generally similar to that used in the earliest clippers, the main difference being a change in deck levels which brought the tiller above the exposed deck and aft of the rudder post.

The limited distance between the rudder post and the transom or counter necessitated a much shorter tiller which was made of iron. The illustration shows the most common arrangement, whereby the action is transmitted via fixed rollers (or pulley blocks) above the tiller level, then to the ship's sides and back to each side of the tiller. Sometimes a metal quadrant was used instead of a tiller arm.

All this gear above deck level was an encumbrance and restricted working space on deck, and was consequently covered over by a raised platform of portable gratings which completely filled the stern as far as the wheel, or sometimes just forward of it, with the wheel working in a slotted opening. The barrel was covered with a short curved-top box like an American pillar box. Some American ships with deeper poops retained the old style wooden tiller forward of the rudder post and below a raised poop deck, with the wheel situated in front of the house in a sheltered position. The *Challenge* of 1851 had this arrangement.

The drawback in all these arrangements was that the rope gear always had a certain amount of slack which allowed any very sudden shock on the rudder to be transmitted to the wheel. Considerable deck space was also necessary, and with the designers' tendency to make the poop counters shorter and rounder, inventors experimented with more simple mechanical gears which would occupy the minimum of space and make wheel operation easier.

In the 1840s many such ideas came out and by the 50s had resolved into a more or less common idea of a strong metal yoke, keyed directly on the rudder post head and actuated by two arms which moved in opposite directions from a common shaft with opposed threads. The basic idea had been patented in 1834 by John Rapson but with the opposed threads on two separate shafts. Rapson was later responsible for a strong power-operated steering gear on the old tiller principle used on steam warships for many years.

The advantages of the worm geared system were a considerable saving in deck space, a direct positive action, and the absence of sudden shocks felt at the helm, since the worm gear could not 'walk back' from pressure on the rudder. The rudder post yoke or crosshead could be placed under the middle or one end of the gear, usually the latter since an emergency tiller was often kept on the rudder in readiness. The whole gear was

STEERING GEARS *HAND OPERATED*

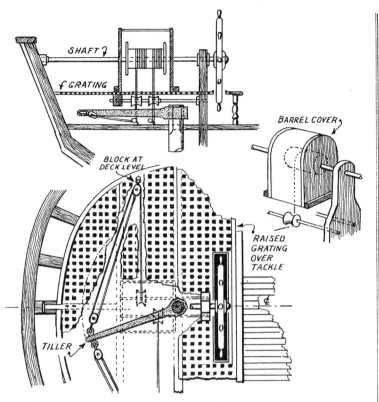

TILLER WITH TACKLE TO BARREL

SHAFT

GRATING

BARREL COVER

BLOCK AT DECK LEVEL

RAISED GRATING OVER TACKLE

TILLER

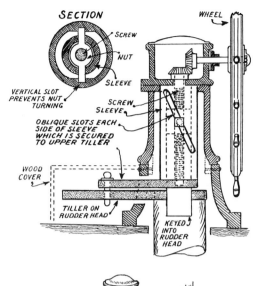

SECTION

WHEEL

SCREW

NUT

SLEEVE

VERTICAL SLOT PREVENTS NUT TURNING

SCREW SLEEVE

OBLIQUE SLOTS EACH SIDE OF SLEEVE WHICH IS SECURED TO UPPER TILLER

WOOD COVER

TILLER ON RUDDER HEAD

KEYED INTO RUDDER HEAD

PILLAR BOX TYPE

WHEEL ACTUATES VERTICAL SCREW WITH BEVEL GEARS WHICH MOVES NUT VERTICALLY. PEGS ON NUT MOVE IN OBLIQUE SLOTS WHICH TURNS SLEEVE CYLINDER AND THE UPPER TILLER. THIS TILLER IS PEGGED AND KEYED TO LOWER TILLER

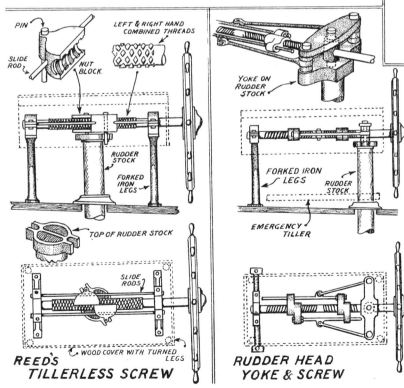

PIN

LEFT & RIGHT HAND COMBINED THREADS

SLIDE ROD

NUT BLOCK

RUDDER STOCK

FORKED IRON LEGS

TOP OF RUDDER STOCK

SLIDE RODS

WOOD COVER WITH TURNED LEGS

REED'S TILLERLESS SCREW

YOKE ON RUDDER STOCK

FORKED IRON LEGS

RUDDER STOCK

EMERGENCY TILLER

RUDDER HEAD YOKE & SCREW

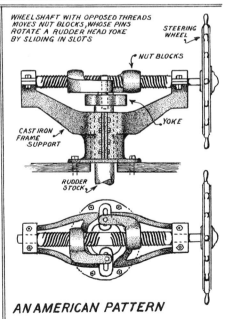

WHEELSHAFT WITH OPPOSED THREADS MOVES NUT BLOCKS, WHOSE PINS ROTATE A RUDDER HEAD YOKE BY SLIDING IN SLOTS

STEERING WHEEL

NUT BLOCKS

YOKE

CAST IRON FRAME SUPPORT

RUDDER STOCK

AN AMERICAN PATTERN

[45]

supported by strong iron legs or a heavy frame, and if close enough to a strong taffrail could be bolted to this also. A wooden rectangular wheel box with sloping lids like a skylight, and ornamental legs, was placed over the somewhat unsightly arrangement.

One ingenious arrangement known as the pillar box steering gear, from its resemblance to a Victorian style British pillar box, was fitted vertically over the rudder post and occupied the minimum of space, an advantage to designers aiming for the shortest counters. Details of this can be seen in the illustration, for which I am indebted to the late Mr A D Edwardes of Australia.

With all steering gear types there was always a spare tiller either stowed away or on the post, and eyebolts about the deck ready to take relieving tackle.

Up to the 19th century naval ships brought in the anchor cable (hemp) by means of a capstan operated on one or two decks, this also being the only machine for moving or hoisting any heavy weights. Merchant ships also had capstans, somewhat smaller and chiefly used for warping into berths. The anchor cable was brought in by means of a windlass, a long horizontal barrel operated by handspikes inserted into holes. This barrel, in small ships, was secured at each end in heavy sockets built against the bulwarks, and in larger ships in sockets or holes in heavy wooden posts (carrick bitts) which had strong knees to the deck on their forward sides.

Chain cables had been in use since the first decade of the 19th century, with studded links on some of the larger Indiamen, and by the advent of the American clippers were in common use.

With the ship at anchor the strain on the cable was taken by the turns on the windlass barrel which was prevented from unwinding by a heavy iron plate ratchet (pawl) from another strong post, which dropped by gravity into an iron cogged rim around the middle of the barrel. Sometimes there were up to three of these pawls of varying lengths above one another. The windlass thus could only operate normally in one direction, bringing the cable aboard and not letting it go. When a ship was coming to anchor an estimate had to be made beforehand of the approximate length of cable required and this was brought up from the cable locker. The end of the cable was led over the top of the windlass barrel from aft with two complete turns and then forward through the hawse pipe and shackled to the anchor ring. The full length of required cable had now to be pulled around the windlass drum and laid along the deck in long loops until the turns around the windlass were at the end of the required length, or as nearly so as could be estimated. When the anchor was let go, the cable along the deck would run out until it was stopped by the turns around the windlass, which were left slack to avoid a sudden shock. Any additional length required had to be eased around the drum by means of long hooks, and additional hooks with two prongs were hooked onto links of the cable and attached to an eyebolt on the centre pawl bitt to help ease the strain on the windlass when riding at anchor.

The wooden windlass drum had iron whelps around it which were renewable and varied in shape, their purpose being to protect the wood and also grip the cable. Sometimes the last length of cable might pull around the windlass in a shower of sparks before being held tight, and when this happened it was necessary to keep the turns around the windlass free of each other, otherwise they could override, jam and possibly break. To prevent this, stout iron bar hoops called normans were inserted into holes in the upper whelps, straddling each separate turn. The hoops and the windlass remained stationary, locked by the pawl.

The period of the 1830s and 1840s was prolific in the invention of

Chapter Eleven

Windlass and Forecastle Arrangement

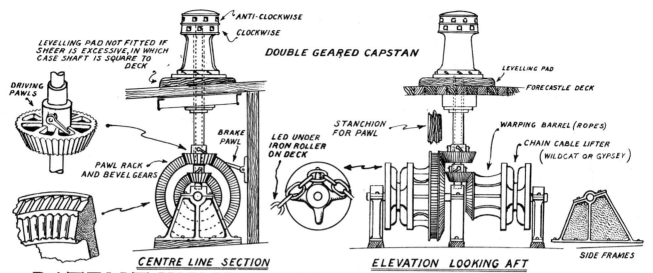

PATENT WINDLASS - EMERSON WALKER TYPE

The capstan can be single geared direct drive to windlass. A number of variations were made with more elaborate gearing arrangements and a brake drum. The main pawl could also operate from a deck fitting without a post

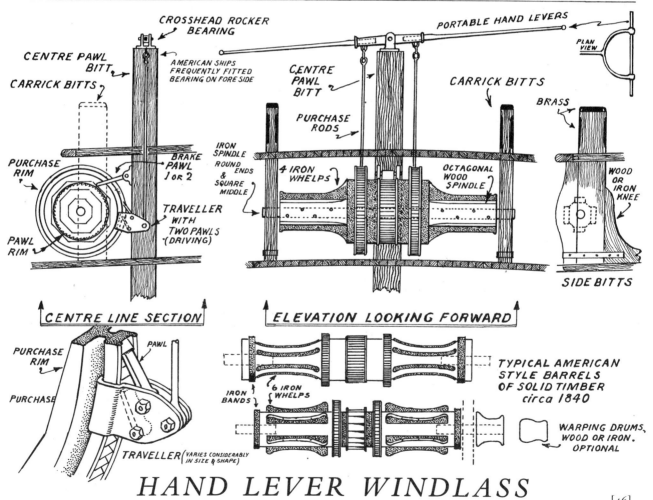

HAND LEVER WINDLASS

mechanical gadgets for ships. By about 1832 the old method for turning the windlass drum by handspikes was improved upon, no doubt because of the increasing use of chain cable. This was effected by an invention whereby two travellers with ratchets turned iron cogged rims each side of the pawl rim, by alternately moving up and down, the motion being supplied by thwartships hand levers pulling purchase rods (46). This arrangement remained in common use for large ships until the late 1850s, and indeed into the present century on some vessels. Other closely similar ideas followed, including one in which each traveller was rotated by pulling on levers rather like the old handspikes but without the necessity of withdrawing them after each pull. Some of the larger American clippers increased the manpower of the thwartship hand lever type by using a short centre bitt with the crosshead rocker close to the forecastle deck level. From the crosshead a long iron shaft ran along the deck in bearings and from it about three additional sets of levers were angled upwards, thereby enabling more men to operate it.

About the same time that the hand lever windlass with traveller came into use, cable compressors were introduced as an improvement on the chain hooks to hold the cable in addition to the windlass. These were heavy iron pads with grooves along their centres, fixed to the deck just inside the hawse holes or pipes. The chain cable led over the pad and could be locked in place by dropping a thick, hinged iron bar over the flat of a link and into a slot.

The final design of windlass was thought out in general principle by John Avery in 1855, but brought into production by two well known manufacturers Harfield and Emerson Walker in 1858–60. It was operated by a capstan with bevel gears (Avery's had levers on a vertical shaft), and the old wooden barrel was replaced by strong metal cable lifters over which the cable fitted snugly into shaped recesses. The earliest form is shown on the drawing of the patent windlass and was considerably elaborated later by the addition of friction brake drums and eventually by a steam-powered drive from a donkey boiler. This, however, was just after the end of the British tea clipper period. The American tea clippers kept to the wooden barrel type as they were out of the trade by the time the patent windlass was in vogue.

With the older form of wooden windlass, the anchor cable led some distance aft along the deck, perhaps as far as the forward deckhouse, and then went down to the cable locker in the hold through a chain or navel pipe. The deck planking under the lead of the cable was thickened or covered with sheathing boards. The patent metal windlass sometimes had this arrangement also, but as the cable only led over the gypsy once, it was held down on it by passing under an iron deck roller just aft of the windlass. When the patent metal windlass was used the more usual arrangement was to have the navel pipe immediately under the gypsy so that the cable went over the top and then straight down to a chain locker situated nearer the bow.

The iron and composite clippers introduced watertight plate bulkheads at the bow and stern, the foremost one, the collision bulkhead, serving as one side of a chain locker. Ships with very fine fore ends would endeavour to have the weighty chain lockers as far from the bow as convenient.

The arrangement of the forecastle deck was largely dependent on the position of the windlass, and the width of the windlass drums was in turn dependent on the distance apart of the hawseholes, which varied according to the bow being full or fine lined. Contemporary builders' drawings can sometimes be at fault here, as being drawn before the ship was built any necessary modifications were made on the ship during the building and not necessarily altered on the drawings. Reproduction of plans by blueprinting was unknown until the last quarter of the 19th century. An original would be made on white paper and any copies had to be hand-traced on transparent linen. Naval dockyards could afford this sort of work but it is not likely that smaller shipyards could. One shipyard in which my father worked in the 1890s producing steel-hulled four-masters and smaller steam vessels, had one man who constituted designer, estimator, and draughtsman, and so much for inherited skill, he was Swiss. Within the outline of the basic general arrangement that he produced, each foreman or tradesman in the yard used his own initiative and experience to produce a workable ship, but it was seldom that the plan was brought up to date with the final solutions. The larger yards producing ocean-going steamships would have more drawing office personnel of course, although even here one comes across builders' drawings which do not tally entirely with contemporary photographs, even allowing for later alterations.

To revert to the arrangement of the windlass and the forecastle, the conditions to be satisfied were that there should be sufficient space to walk around the capstan, and to stand each side of the hand levers for the windlass, which resulted in some odd shapes for the anchor deck. The arrangement on the *Vision*, for instance, gave a semicircular convex end to the deck, the capstan being on the forecastle deck and the windlass operating from the upper deck, the centre pawl bitt being short in consequence (22). Other ships had the reverse, whereby a concave shaped end to the forecastle deck and a longer centre pawl bitt enabled both windlass and capstan to be operated from the forecastle deck.

Some of these short anchor decks were only three or four feet high being little more than a platform with barely enough space to crawl under, and with this arrangement the body of the windlass barrel was exposed

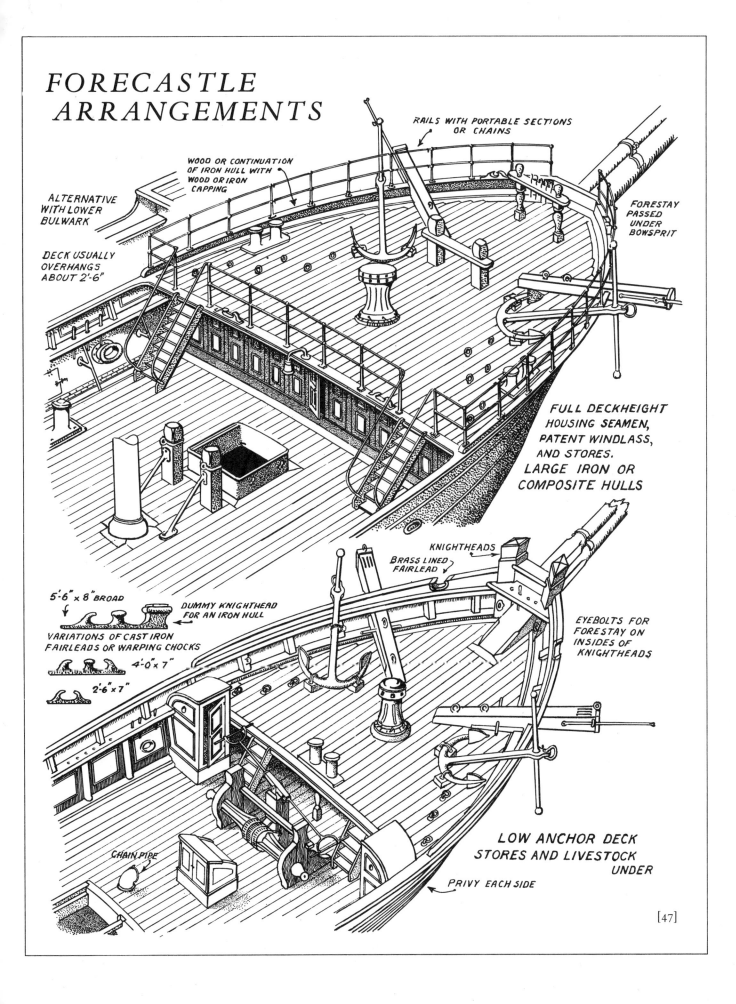

FORECASTLE ARRANGEMENTS

RAILS WITH PORTABLE SECTIONS OR CHAINS

WOOD OR CONTINUATION OF IRON HULL WITH WOOD OR IRON CAPPING

ALTERNATIVE WITH LOWER BULWARK

DECK USUALLY OVERHANGS ABOUT 2'-6"

FORESTAY PASSED UNDER BOWSPRIT

FULL DECKHEIGHT HOUSING SEAMEN, PATENT WINDLASS, AND STORES.
LARGE IRON OR COMPOSITE HULLS

KNIGHTHEADS

BRASS LINED FAIRLEAD

5'-6" x 8" BROAD

DUMMY KNIGHTHEAD FOR AN IRON HULL

VARIATIONS OF CAST IRON FAIRLEADS OR WARPING CHOCKS

4'-0" x 7"

2'-6" x 7"

EYEBOLTS FOR FORESTAY ON INSIDES OF KNIGHTHEADS

CHAIN PIPE

LOW ANCHOR DECK
STORES AND LIVESTOCK UNDER

PRIVY EACH SIDE

[47]

FORECASTLE ARRANGEMENTS

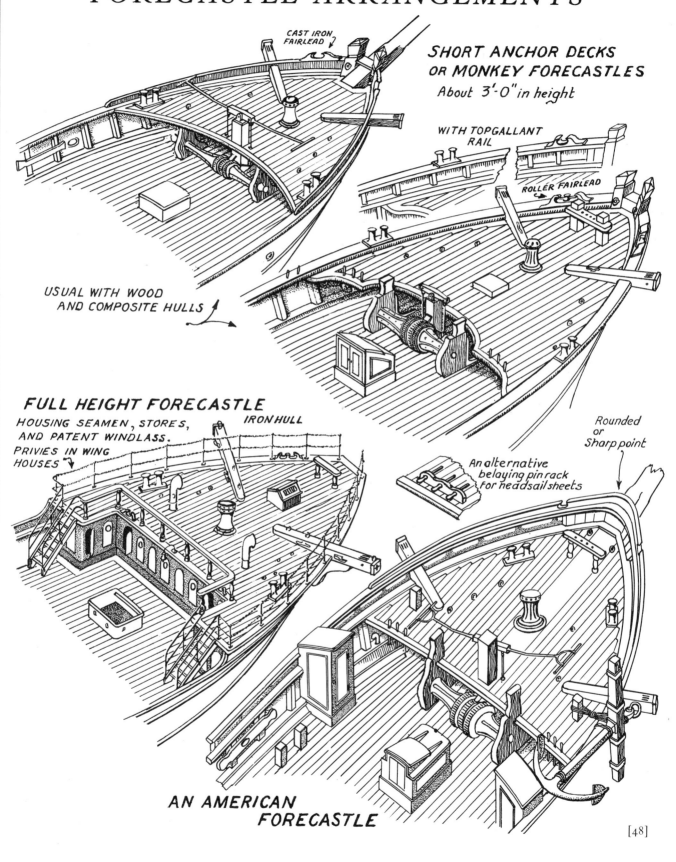

CAST IRON FAIRLEAD

SHORT ANCHOR DECKS
OR **MONKEY FORECASTLES**
About 3'-0" in height

WITH TOPGALLANT RAIL

ROLLER FAIRLEAD

USUAL WITH WOOD
AND COMPOSITE HULLS ↑

FULL HEIGHT FORECASTLE
HOUSING SEAMEN, STORES,
AND PATENT WINDLASS.
PRIVIES IN WING
HOUSES ↘

IRON HULL

Rounded or Sharp point

An alternative belaying pin rack for headsail sheets

AN AMERICAN FORECASTLE

so that it could be attended to, either completely clear of the deck or with the three bitts built as support into the end of the deck.

The drawings of forecastle arrangements give the most common arrangements met with in the tea clippers (47, 48). With the capstan-operated patent windlass the forecastle deck was higher, at least head height, and under it were storerooms or possibly accommodation. A capstan showing a double rim of holes for bars indicated a patent mechanical windlass below, and this capstan had a flat domed top. The capstan for warping only was smaller and had a higher domed top with only one rim of holes.

It was not usual to fit rails or stanchions on the shallow forecastle decks, or even ladders, although there were some exceptions with wooden stanchions and rail. The higher full deck height forecastles did fit metal rails and stanchions and ladders, the rails being either solid iron bars or light chains tightened at one end by a rope lanyard. In either case the stanchions and rails were portable, detachable or hinged in the area where the anchor would swing inboard for stowage.

The main rail of the bulwark ran to the stem with the smaller type of forecastle deck and also formed its margin plank. The thwartships margin plank was always raised a little proud of the forecastle deck planking, about $\frac{3}{4}$ in., to form a waterway to small lead scuppers at each side, as whenever possible on sailing ships clean deck space was utilized in rain showers to replenish the main fresh water tanks.

The large wooden catheads were set off as square as possible to the deck and bolted down to the deck over a heavy beam on the underside, the catbeam. If the deck was fairly wide the jib-boom guys would lead to the cathead and be secured with deadeyes or hearts and lanyards. With a very narrow forecastle deck, in order to give a more efficient spread to these guys, hinged iron bars (whisker booms) were attached to the ends of the catheads, and the jib-boom stays or guys led over a fork or cleat at the end and then attached to the hull just aft of the cathead. This would especially be the case with flying jib-booms. The whisker boom would hinge upwards to clear obstructions when docking.

As indicated on the drawing of anchors, there were two main types fitted in the tea clippers, wooden stocked and iron stocked (49). The former, which dated back centuries but with more angular arms, was mostly favoured in America, and some Down Easters of the 1890s still carried them. Evidence from photographs indicates that occasionally both British and American clippers carried one of each type on opposite sides. American stocks were commonly rounded in a barrel shaped taper, or left square on the centre portion and octagonal beyond that, whereas the British pattern had squared corners and a taper on the lower side. The wooden stock was made in two halves which in earlier times were un-

ANCHORS
SOME TYPICAL ANCHORS OF 1850

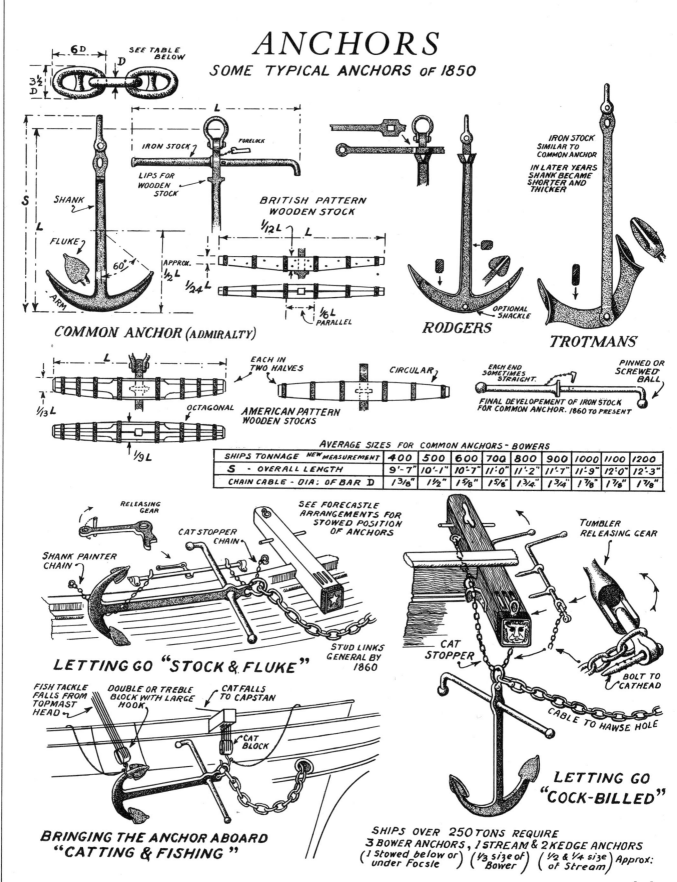

SHIPS TONNAGE NEW MEASUREMENT	400	500	600	700	800	900	1000	1100	1200
S - OVERALL LENGTH	9'-7"	10'-1"	10'-7"	11'-0"	11'-2"	11'-7"	11'-9"	12'-0"	12'-3"
CHAIN CABLE - DIA: OF BAR D	1 3/8"	1 1/2"	1 5/8"	1 5/8"	1 3/4"	1 3/4"	1 7/8"	1 7/8"	1 7/8"

AVERAGE SIZES FOR COMMON ANCHORS - BOWERS

COMMON ANCHOR (ADMIRALTY)

RODGERS

TROTMANS

AMERICAN PATTERN WOODEN STOCKS

FINAL DEVELOPEMENT OF IRON STOCK FOR COMMON ANCHOR. 1860 TO PRESENT

LETTING GO "STOCK & FLUKE"

LETTING GO "COCK-BILLED"

BRINGING THE ANCHOR ABOARD "CATTING & FISHING"

SHIPS OVER 250 TONS REQUIRE
3 BOWER ANCHORS, 1 STREAM & 2 KEDGE ANCHORS
(1 stowed below or under Focsle) (1/3 size of Bower) (1/2 & 1/4 size of Stream) Approx:

shipped at sea and stowed away. The type of wooden stock which had an upward curve, sometimes seen in maritime museums' gardens today, was a European style but occasionally found its way onto British ships, probably as a replacement. The proportions of different makes of anchor varied, as weight was the criterion, the tendency over the years being to make them shorter and thicker. The common anchor with its easily removable iron stock was the most popular. At first the stock had two straight sides and could be unshipped completely at sea. Later, with the tip of one side bent, it could be withdrawn partially and lashed alongside the shank. Anchors were best stowed across the deck, with the stock vertical against the side of the hull if it was not withdrawn completely. The third bower anchor was stowed in any convenient position, sometimes vertically in a slot in the forecastle deck near the after edge, the arms being uppermost. To move the anchor about for stowing or into a position for letting go, a heavy tackle (fish tackle) was suspended from a pendant from the fore topmast hounds. The large hook on the lower block was triced up to the foot of the forestay when not in use in coastal waters, but on a long voyage the tackle would be stowed away.

The older method of letting go the anchor 'cock-billed' was to suspend it below the cathead with a chain (cat stopper) one end of which had some releasing arrangement such as a slip link or a pin through a link which could be knocked out with a mallet. This could be dangerous as the end of the chain might fly out and whip back again, so a safer method was devised with a tumbler releasing pin operated by a remote lever. In either case a man would have to go over the side beforehand to release the fish tackle hook from the shank of the anchor or from a ring on a gravity band on the shank. This operation was in turn eliminated by preparing the anchor for letting go by the 'catting and fishing' system, whereby the anchor was held horizontally to a releasing bar with a chain at each end, the shank painter and the cat stopper. Several varieties of releasing gear were invented, the one shown being typical (49). In all cases the two chains were led from their fixed inboard ends under the anchor or the ring, and then over and back to the release pegs, so that when released they flew outwards and downwards clear of the operator.

To bring the anchor aboard it was always necessary, once it was hanging from the hawsehole clear of the water, for a man to go overside in order to hook on the fish tackle; an operation carried out by an experienced hand owing to its danger. It was not until the introduction of stockless anchors, which could be hauled up into the hawsepipe and left there, that the man overside became unnecessary, although this was after the clipper ship era; and in fact the stockless anchor did not appear on the late windjammers even though it was common on steamships at the time.

Chapter Twelve

Boats

The number of boats to be supplied to a merchant ship was not fixed by law and was left to the discretion of the owner up to the time of the Merchant Shipping Act of 1854, when it was specified that boats should be adequate to the number of persons aboard. Lloyd's Rules are concerned with the safety of the ship as a whole, it being left to civil authorities to protect the safety of individuals aboard, and they simply required at that time an adequate number of boats of good quality. The Liverpool rules for iron ships by the 1860s called for three boats (lifeboat, pinnace and gig) for ships of over 400 tons, which was the minimum usually found on the tea clippers. The larger American clippers, built to take passengers, carried up to five boats.

The largest boat, dating back from naval practice, was the longboat or launch. This was carvel built, possibly diagonal or double skinned, of a length between 30 and 42 ft and proportions of length divided by beam between $3\frac{1}{2}$ to 4. The launch of the American *Challenge* was somewhat narrower at $26 \times 9 \times 3$ ft 6 in. with 12 oars. The longboat, heavily built with sawn timbers like a ship, usually had removable thwarts and could stow another small boat inside it if necessary. Its use was for transporting stores, water, etc. or occasionally laying out an anchor, but when stowed on deck advantage was taken of its size by filling it with livestock pens, and even surrounding it by a portable set of rails to confine livestock on the deck. A number of American ships used to berth the longboat inside a long deckhouse of which the after sides and end were removable so that the boat could be moved into the open on rollers. The British clipper *Vision* had this arrangement but it was a rarity on British ships. The longboat was too large to be suspended from davits and was launched by tackle from yardarms or a special strong stay slung between the fore and main masts, called a triatic stay. It carried between 10 and 12 oars which could be shipped in semicircular metal crutches; with wooden thole pins; or in metal-lined notches which were cut into an additional wash strake above the sheerstrake and gunwale.

Other boats were:

Cutter	22–32 ft	$L \div B = 3\frac{1}{2}$ to 4	6 to 8 oars, clinker built
Jolly boat	16–22 ft	$L \div B = 3$ to $3\frac{1}{2}$	clinker built
Yawl	23–30 ft	$L \div B = 3\frac{1}{2}$ to 4	carvel built
Dinghy	12–14 ft	$L \div B = 3$	clinker built
Gig	22–28 ft	$L \div B = 4\frac{1}{2}$ to 5	clinker built
Lifeboat	24–30 ft	$L \div B = 3\frac{1}{2}$ to 4	clinker built

The average equipment for a composite clipper would be a longboat on deck, or a gig on the deckhouse with two lifeboats on skids with possibly a small jolly boat between them. The lifeboats were double ended, as also at times the yawl, all others having transom sterns of varying fullness.

Davits were fitted each side on the after quarters for quarterboats which

BOATS

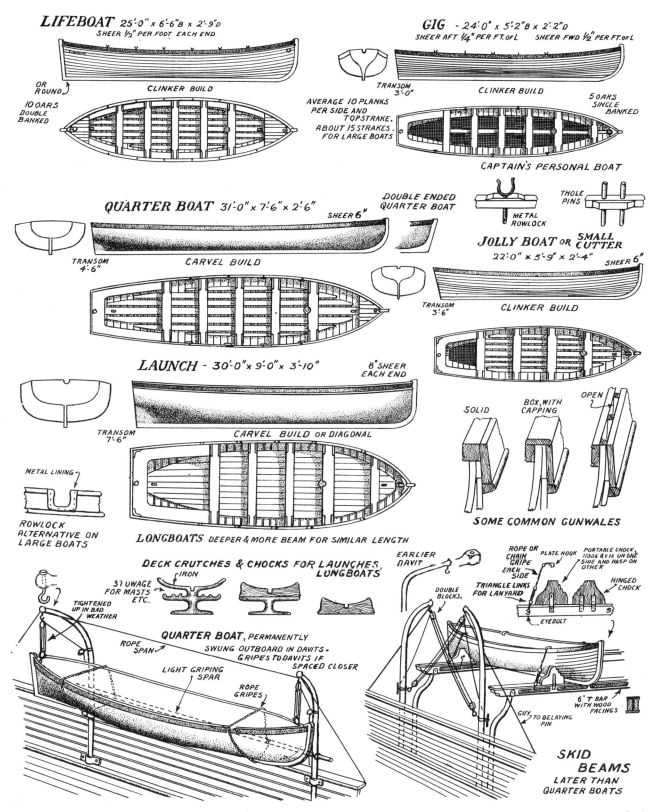

LIFEBOAT 25'-0" x 6'-6"B x 2'-9"D
SHEER 1/2" PER FOOT EACH END

CLINKER BUILD

OR ROUND

10 OARS DOUBLE BANKED

GIG - 24'-0" x 5'-2"B x 2'-2"D
SHEER AFT 1/4" PER FT. OF L   SHEER FWD 1/2" PER FT. OF L

TRANSOM 3'-0"

CLINKER BUILD

AVERAGE 10 PLANKS PER SIDE AND TOPSTRAKE. ABOUT 15 STRAKES FOR LARGE BOATS

5 OARS SINGLE BANKED

CAPTAIN'S PERSONAL BOAT

QUARTER BOAT 31'-0" x 7'-6" x 2'-6"   SHEER 6"

DOUBLE ENDED QUARTER BOAT

TRANSOM 4'-6"   CARVEL BUILD

THOLE PINS

METAL ROWLOCK

JOLLY BOAT OR **SMALL CUTTER**
22'-0" x 5'-9" x 2'-4"   SHEER 6"

TRANSOM 3'-6"   CLINKER BUILD

LAUNCH - 30'-0" x 9'-0" x 3'-10"   8" SHEER EACH END

TRANSOM 7'-6"   CARVEL BUILD OR DIAGONAL

SOLID   BOX, WITH CAPPING   OPEN

SOME COMMON GUNWALES

METAL LINING

ROWLOCK ALTERNATIVE ON LARGE BOATS

LONGBOATS DEEPER & MORE BEAM FOR SIMILAR LENGTH

DECK CRUTCHES & CHOCKS FOR LAUNCHES, LONGBOATS

IRON

STOWAGE FOR MASTS ETC.

TIGHTENED UP IN BAD WEATHER

QUARTER BOAT, PERMANENTLY SWUNG OUTBOARD IN DAVITS. GRIPES TO DAVITS IF SPACED CLOSER

ROPE SPAN

LIGHT GRIPING SPAR

ROPE GRIPES

EARLIER DAVIT

ROPE OR CHAIN GRIPE EACH SIDE

TRIANGLE LINKS FOR LANYARD

PLATE HOOK

PORTABLE CHOCK HOOK & EYE ON ONE SIDE AND HASP ON OTHER

HINGED CHOCK

EYEBOLT

DOUBLE BLOCKS.

GUY TO BELAYING PIN

6" T BAR WITH WOOD FACINGS

SKID BEAMS LATER THAN QUARTER BOATS

were usually yawls or small cutters if kept permanently hung outboard, as was the case with many of the earlier American clippers and British East Indiamen. Later, stronger davits would be fitted for two lifeboats on the skid beams. Quarterboats were not so vulnerable as would appear at first sight when swung outboard, although there were occasions when they did go by the board, as did boats stowed on chocks on the deck or on skid beams. The quarterboat davits were weak in design in the 1840s and '50s, resembling in shape a straight round bar, bent rather sharply in the top portion. Later davits had the quarter-circle radius bend, as seen today, and were stronger. The earliest type of davit tackle hung from a simple swivel hook from the ball at the end of the davit, and the guy and span attached below the ball could get tangled if the davit was swung round. The tip of the early davits was sometimes merely a slight swelling in the diameter with a vertical hole for the hooked bolt, or else a cube shape with corners rounded off. It was late in the century before the spectacle plate was fixed atop the ball, for the guys and span to prevent this fouling.

The boat gripes for quarterboats were rope spans attached to the lower part of the davits then led under the boat, over the gunwales, and down to an inverted hook on the davit or bulwark. A ring on the end of each gripe slipped over the hook and was held fast when the boat falls were tightened. Sometimes a light griping spar was fitted between the davits, but not of the heavy padded type one sees on modern vessels. In heavy weather the quarterboats would be hove up tight to the davit heads and lashed to them slightly canted.

By the 1860s and '70s lifeboats were stowed either upright or inverted on strong skid beams spanning from bulwark to bulwark, and secured by separate gripes on each side of the boat, with a special sliplink tightened by a lanyard. If stowed upright, the boats would rest in shaped chocks, the outboard part being hinged so that by releasing a locking pin with a mallet it would fall down completely clear of the top of the skid beam, thus enabling the boat to be slid or skidded outboard to the davits. The inboard chock would also hinge down if there was a third, middle, boat on the skids to be slid to the davits. The spacing of the skid beams supported the boats at about one-seventh of their lengths from each end. The davits were the round bar radial type of modern pattern which could be held in sockets either inboard or outboard. At sea the davits would be triced together by their fall tackle, and in coastal waters the boats would usually be swung outboard in readiness.

British boat gunwales were built with a solid top or cap but it was usual for American boats to have open gunwales with the timber heads exposed. The practice of fitting covers on boats dates from the steamships, which emitted much soot and cinders. Sailing vessels usually kept their boats open as this helped preserve them against rot, and any water accumulating inside helped to keep them tight; there was always a drain hole to release any excess. Later in the century we find wooden covers fitted, and canvas ones with a ridge pole, tightened on buttons around the gunwale, although there is mention of the *Challenge* of 1851 being fitted with awnings for her boats. There was no rule about this. The looped grablines were seldom seen on the clipper ships' boats but eventually became a requirement for lifeboats. Up to approximately mid-century the suspension hooks or rings for the boats were on short slings attached to the keel close up to the bow and stern and the boat was prevented from canting by steadying lines from each side of the hull to the sling. Later in the century the sling hooks were on rigid bars not quite so far apart, and supported at their top ends by passing through a short thwart or platform. Sometimes the sling hooks were attached to the upper inner side of the stern and sternpost or transom, and contemporary paintings of the earlier American clippers suggest this in some instances for the quarterboats.

Good boats were made of teak or mahogany planking, or at least their sheerstrakes, with larch, cedar or pine planking. Their proportions and form varied considerably with their origin, some being built in the shipyard and others by small boat builders, and the captain frequently had his own small gig for pleasure sailing. The names given to the various forms of boats originated from their usage rather than a specific build, and it is difficult to identify precisely what was meant by a given name. 'Cutter' in particular was loosely used for a variety of boats which could be carvel or clinker built. American boats tended to be carvel built more often than the British. The drawings indicate average forms, sheer, etc. for British boats; American boats being similar for the most part, although there were some types indigenous to the American builders, with pronounced sheer more like their whaleboats and rather narrower. At one time the term 'cutter built' was synonymous with 'clinker built'.

For other forms of lifesaving there was often a type of lifebuoy carried on the poop for quick release. Up to the 1850s this was in the form of a cross with two copper ball floats on the end of each arm, and a foot stirrup at the bottom whereby a person could stand upright in the water while holding the top part of the cross, which also could carry a small pennant. Later a horseshoe lifebuoy made of cork was introduced, the two arms being hinged at the middle, to which was attached a small staff and pennant, weighted at the bottom to keep it vertical. Later still came the well known circular lifebuoy made of cork, 30 in. in diameter with a cross-section of 6×4 in., covered with stitched canvas; but this type was seldom seen on the tea clippers until later in their life.

Chapter Thirteen

Fife Rails and Bitts

The word 'bitts' originally referred to strong wooden posts which extended through two deck levels for strength, and were usually in pairs, with a heavy cross-member called a horse. They were situated immediately forward of the fore and main masts and were known as jeer (jear) bitts, the jeers being the heavy tackle which suspended the lower yards in the 18th century before the introduction of iron trusses. The lead from the jeer blocks went through a vertical sheave in the bitt (one each side) and was then belayed around the top of the bitt. There were three sheave holes in each bitt, one for the jeers and the others for the topsail sheets and the clew garnets. After the elimination of the jeers the bitts became known as topsail sheet bitts.

The foremast topsail sheet bitts could also be used to ease the strain off the cable on the windlass, by having the cable (rope) also take some turns around the ends of the cross-member. With a chain cable a separate rope or tackle would be hooked or seized to the chain and then belayed around the cross-member. The vertical bitts would have strong knees of wood or iron to the deck if used for this purpose.

The crosspiece was used as a belaying rail and pierced with holes for the belaying pins, the member then being called a fife rail. Centuries before, the fife rail was at the ship's side and referred to a long thick horizontal plank let into the timber heads abreast the mast. It was pierced with belaying pin holes which from its similarity to the musical instrument gave rise to the name. Eventually the bitts on the centreline had additional fife rails in the fore and aft direction and were supported by turned stanchions, in a variety of patterns as shown.(51) The sheaves for topsail sheet etc. were retained on some clippers, but on others the lead blocks were hooked to eyebolts around the mast, and belaying was done on a spider band on the mast which held a number of belaying pins. An elaboration on the arrangement of fife rails which dated back to much earlier times was sometimes made, whereby two additional horizontal rails were added to the sides and ends between the stanchions. A series of swivelling lead blocks with single sheaves were fixed between these rails for various leads of running rigging which were belayed on the top rail. The top rail was then higher than usual, about 4 ft. A small type of single fife rail was often situated on the forecastle just inside the knightheads to belay some of the headsail's running gear.

The mainmast fife rails could take the bearings for the bilge pumps which were normally situated inside the rails, or else the pumps could have their own side frame supports (29). The pump flywheel incidentally had curved spokes, not just for ornament's sake but because it was found that with straight spokes, as the casting cooled down the varying rate of contraction of the spokes as against that of the thick rim often caused cracks in the wheel. (The old-fashioned domestic mangle had similar wheels,

FIFE RAILS and BITTS

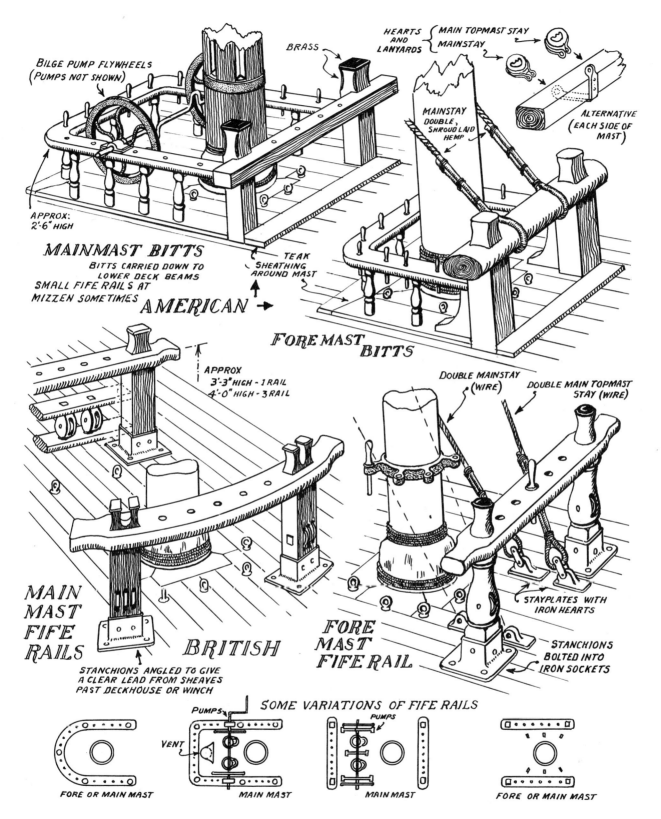

BILGE PUMP FLYWHEELS
(PUMPS NOT SHOWN)

BRASS

HEARTS AND LANYARDS { MAIN TOPMAST STAY
MAINSTAY

ALTERNATIVE
(EACH SIDE OF MAST)

MAINSTAY DOUBLE, SHROUD LAID HEMP

APPROX:
2'-6" HIGH

MAINMAST BITTS
BITTS CARRIED DOWN TO LOWER DECK BEAMS
SMALL FIFE RAILS AT MIZZEN SOMETIMES
AMERICAN →

TEAK SHEATHING AROUND MAST

FOREMAST BITTS

APPROX
3'-3" HIGH - 1 RAIL
4'-0" HIGH - 3 RAIL

DOUBLE MAINSTAY (WIRE)

DOUBLE MAIN TOPMAST STAY (WIRE)

MAIN MAST FIFE RAILS
BRITISH

STANCHIONS ANGLED TO GIVE A CLEAR LEAD FROM SHEAVES PAST DECKHOUSE OR WINCH

FORE MAST FIFE RAIL

STAYPLATES WITH IRON HEARTS

STANCHIONS BOLTED INTO IRON SOCKETS

SOME VARIATIONS OF FIFE RAILS

PUMPS

VENT

FORE OR MAIN MAST

MAIN MAST

PUMPS

MAIN MAST

FORE OR MAIN MAST

[51]

though smaller.) The pump tubes were set so that they landed each side of the keelson, and immediately outboard of them were frequently situated the main fresh water tanks in the hold. A small access hatch to the tanks was then placed just aft of the pumps with a wooden trunk in the 'tween decks to keep it clear of cargo. The hatch could have a portable cowl vent fitted instead of a cover. With fresh water tanks in this area, the small pump required would be secured underneath the after side of the fife rails. However the smaller clippers usually preferred to keep the main hold clear of obstructions and placed a fresh water tank somewhere below the poop deck area where a pump could lead up beside the pantry sink.

On American ships, where wood was used in preference to iron for economy reasons, bitts were situated about the deck for mooring purposes. These were usually in pairs in the fore and aft direction and extended through two deck levels. British ships, however, with the easy availability of iron castings, had the mooring bitts made up of large hollow castings on thick bedplates bolted onto the deck. These were called bollards and often had a screw-down brass dome on top of each 'stump' so that they could act as exhaust ventilators as well. The old style bitts to the fife rails were also cut short at upper deck level and secured in cast iron sockets and were then referred to as stanchions or standards. Sometimes the type of bitt or standard containing sheaves was angled, with the cross-rail in a slight curve. This was done so that men tailing on a rope leading through a sheave could have a path clear of adjacent winches or perhaps the end of a deckhouse.

On American vessels there was also frequently a single bitt each side of the poop approximately abreast the wheel, for belaying boom sheets or for mooring lines. This bitt had a cross-pin either of brass or wood. Although for the most part American bitts were of wood, spanning two decks, there is some evidence that in our period metal bollards were occasionally used.

For belaying running rigging at the ship's side abreast the masts, there were a number of different methods. The commonest was to increase the width of the main rail to accommodate the pins, which were then sheltered by the height of bulwark to the topgallant rail above it. If no topgallant rail was fitted, as on some of the smaller British clippers, a pin rail was let into the face of the bulwark stanchions below the main rail level. This pin rail was usually continuous from the forecastle deck to near the turn of the stern on the flush-decked ships. On ships with a raised quarter deck or poop deck the mizzen running rigging belayed on a separate single fife rail on wood or metal stanchions situated just inside the poop rails and stanchions, or if a substantial wooden poop rail was fitted, it was pierced for belaying pins also. Some flush-decked American ships carried a small fife rail at the mizzen.

Another method was to fit a strong wooden or iron pin rail, with bosses pierced with holes, across the insides of the mizzen lower shrouds just above the level of the deadeyes, to which it was securely seized. It was of a thickness, and with grooves on the outer face, such that it would not twist or cant with strain on the pins.

The two bitts forward of the foremast on later British iron ships were sometimes made as stout iron tube ventilators to the hold, to which the mainstay also attached to eyes smithed on bands. American ships also favoured the setting up of the mainstays to the crosspiece of the foremast bitts, either with hearts and lanyards to iron straps or seized directly around the timber itself. In earlier years when the foremast was further forward, the mainstay attached to the windlass pawl bitt, first passing under a cleat on the side of the foremast to bring the stay closer to the deck and clear of the foot of the fore course.

Chapter Fourteen

Decking

As one of the most noticeable items on a ship is the deck planking, it is useful to consider some of the factors which governed the laying of the decks on wooden ships or iron composite ones.

In a wooden ship the deck planking was a major item in contributing to the longitudinal strength to resist hogging etc., particularly the waterway and margin plank immediately adjacent to it. These two members therefore were kept large in section and continuous for the full length of the ship and of approximately constant width. A slight decrease in the width was permissible near the extremities but it was a gradual decrease.

At approximately the width of the hatchways additional thick binding strakes were laid full fore and aft, without being pierced for pumps or any other items. The extra thickness of these strakes, possibly one or two each side, was accommodated by their being scored down over the beams until flush with the normal decking, thus locking into all the beams, or else laid flush over the beams at a slightly raised height. In the latter case the deck planking between the binding strakes, down the middle of the deck, would also be increased in thickness, allowing for camber, so that pools of water could not lie against the binding strakes.

The binding strakes were laid in a slightly curved line which was approximately parallel to the deck line for the major length of the ship before the deck commenced to curve in towards the bow or stern. Between the binding strakes and the margin planks, the normal thickness of planking was also laid parallel to them, or in some instances slightly tapering towards the extremities so that the outermost strake ran as long a length as possible. This was in order to get the maximum strength out of long continuous strakes near the ship's side.

The inside edge of the margin plank (which was frequently scored down over the beams) was left in a continuous unbroken curved line.

At the extremities of each plank, to avoid running into a long thin point which could not be efficiently caulked or fastened, the end was cut square, at such a width (approximately $2\frac{1}{2}$ in.) that a caulking iron could be used across it and a hole for a treenail drilled into it near its end without weakening the plank too much. This meant that the next adjacent plank inboard had to be notched around the square end of the previous plank and so on, until the plank ends met the curve at about 30°, which could be effectively caulked and fastened.

The planking down the middle of the deck was not so important, as it was in short lengths, being broken by hatches, scuttles, mast partners, etc. These openings were bounded by vertical coamings (hatch sides) and ledges (ends of hatches). The coamings bolted onto the carling pieces between the beams at the level of the top of beams. The ledges bolted down into a bevelled score across the butt ends of the deck planks which ran to the actual opening in the deck. If the beams at each end of the hatch had

DECK PLANKING

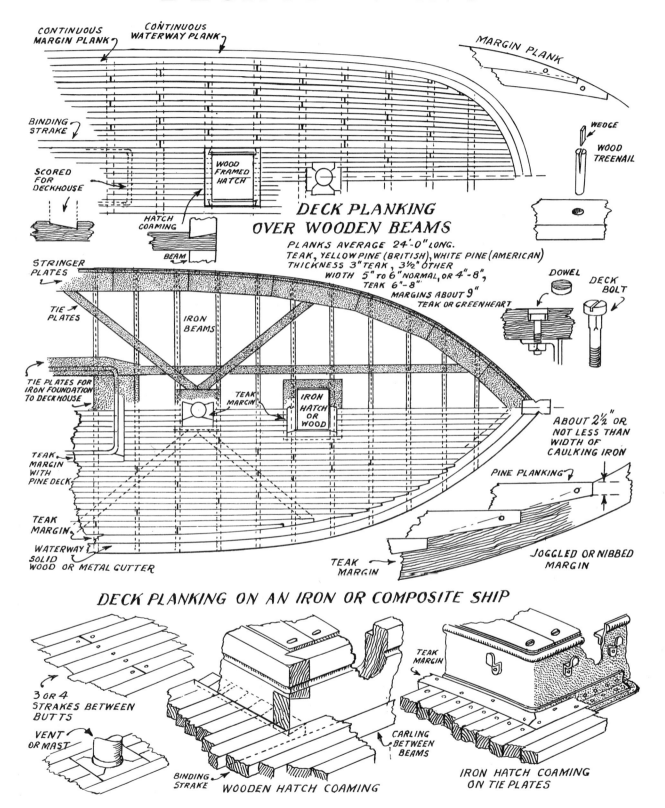

CONTINUOUS MARGIN PLANK

CONTINUOUS WATERWAY PLANK

MARGIN PLANK

BINDING STRAKE

SCORED FOR DECKHOUSE

WOOD FRAMED HATCH

WEDGE

WOOD TREENAIL

HATCH COAMING

BEAM

DECK PLANKING OVER WOODEN BEAMS

PLANKS AVERAGE 24'-0" LONG.
TEAK, YELLOWPINE (BRITISH), WHITE PINE (AMERICAN)
THICKNESS 3" TEAK, 3½" OTHER
WIDTH 5" TO 6" NORMAL, OR 4"-8",
TEAK 6"-8"
MARGINS ABOUT 9"
TEAK OR GREENHEART

STRINGER PLATES

TIE PLATES

IRON BEAMS

DOWEL

DECK BOLT

TIE PLATES FOR IRON FOUNDATION TO DECKHOUSE

TEAK MARGIN

IRON HATCH OR WOOD

ABOUT 2½" OR NOT LESS THAN WIDTH OF CAULKING IRON

TEAK MARGIN WITH PINE DECK

PINE PLANKING

TEAK MARGIN

WATERWAY SOLID WOOD OR METAL GUTTER

TEAK MARGIN

JOGGLED OR NIBBED MARGIN

DECK PLANKING ON AN IRON OR COMPOSITE SHIP

3 OR 4 STRAKES BETWEEN BUTTS

VENT OR MAST

TEAK MARGIN

BINDING STRAKE

WOODEN HATCH COAMING

CARLING BETWEEN BEAMS

IRON HATCH COAMING ON TIE PLATES

sufficient width, the hatch ledges would bed down onto them directly, as also the ends of the planks which would butt up against the ledges.

Under the deckhouses the deck planking was continuous, and a shallow bevelled score was let in to the outline of the deckhouse foundation cants, which enabled the house to be bolted down and lightly caulked or payed. Margin pieces could be fitted around the masts as the partners and chocks below gave sufficient foundation for plank end fastenings as well as the margin.

The treenail fastenings for deck planks were driven down into the beams and then tightened by hardwood wedges, the whole being cut off flush with the deck. The fastenings, being end grain wood, did not wear away as soon as the surrounding deck, and on an old ship would project as rounded humps until planed or adzed down. Sometimes iron spike nails were used instead of treenails, sunk into shallow drilled holes to allow for dowel plugs to seal them.

With an iron or composite ship the decking procedure was different in principle. The strength of the deck and its contribution to the longitudinal strength of the ship was basically in the ironwork structure. The side sheerstrake and deck stringer plate and angle took the place of the wooden waterway and margin plank in giving strength, although the latter were often applied in addition. The wooden binding strakes were replaced by flat iron tie plates running fore and aft, and the whole braced together with diagonal tie plates. The deck planking itself was not so important for longitudinal strength, and the outermost planks did not need to be carried so far forward in a curve as on the wooden ship. The sharp ends of the planks meeting the curve were still cut off square for the caulking iron, but the notching or joggling was cut out of the margin plank instead of the deck planks. If the deck line did have pronounced curvature, the outermost planks could have some curvature and taper to avoid a long narrow plank, but as soon as possible inboard of this the planks would be laid down in straight parallel lines.

Varying rules are given for the length of the sniped taper and square tip for planks finishing on a curve, which are based on proportions to the width of plank, but as planks could vary on occasions from say 4 to 8 in. in width (teak planks could go up to 9 in.), this could result in too much being unnecessarily cut into the margin plank. The principle was that the square end need only accommodate the caulking iron at about $2\frac{1}{2}$ in. with the taper running from this point to the normal width of the margin. As soon as the planks met the curve at about 30° there was no need to square off the tip.

The openings, hatches, etc. were bounded by wide metal tie plates athwartships and fore and aft, and the metal coamings connected to them by angle irons. A margin plank was then laid down around the coaming in teak or pine slightly thicker than the deck and tapered down to deck level; the normal deck planking was butted against the margin with its ends fastened to the tie plate. This would apply also to the metal coamings on companions, ventilators, deckhouses, etc.

If the deck was laid in pine the margins would be teak for good class work as this resisted rust stains from the metal. Even with wooden coamings bolted directly to the tie plates for hatches or deckhouses it was usual to fit teak margins around them as these vertical surfaces caused more water to accumulate than elsewhere and set up rot. With a completely teak deck the margins were not so essential except for appearance, and the deckhouse was usually set into scores in continuous planking.

Teak pads about 2 in. thick were laid under the iron bollards, the patent windlass and the winches; also the area around the masts and under the fife rails was raised similarly with teak sheathing boards.

The sides of topgallant forecastle decks and the break of forecastle and poop decks sometimes had teak covering boards about 1 in. thick with a bevelled or rounded edge. This was cheaper than fitting a full depth teak margin. The butt ends of the planking at the exposed deck edge were then covered by a half-round moulding.

On pine decked ships, in order to have a teak margin around a deckhouse without its foundation cutting the planks and bedding on the beams directly, a good method was to fit margin planks about 2 in. thick which were let into the pine deck about 1 in. The extra thickness standing proud above the pine deck could then be either sloped down or rounded off. Water running or dripping down a deckhouse side tended to set up rot or leaking seams and the extra thickness or slope helped in this respect.

The fastenings for a wood deck on iron tie plates or beams were metal bolts with nuts on the underside. The bolt heads were sunk below the surface to permit a wood dowel to be let in flush with the deck. The grain in the dowel was horizontal so that it wore down evenly with the deck, as against the treenail head on the wooden ship which did not. Adjoining butt ends could each have fastening bolts with a vee'd caulking joint, or have one butt sloped vertically to hold down the next plank, or a single bolt through an overlapping half step. The latter arrangement did not leave much substance in the top plank, however, and was weak when there was much strain on the fastening.

A naval officer once told me of an occasion when he was on the bridge of a light cruiser in the Mediterranean during a storm, with the ship labouring and straining heavily. Suddenly a deck plank sprang up from the foredeck, burst all its fastenings and disappeared upwards as though catapulted. This was a sheathing plank, which was laid over a completely steel plated deck, and the incident gives some idea of the strain to which plank fastenings may be subjected.

Chapter Fifteen

Rudders

The type of rudder in general use by the time of the first tea clippers was known as 'gunstock'. The axis of the pintles in this type is in the same line as the centre of the rudder stock, so that when the rudder swings from side to side the stock revolves about its own axis and consequently can be fitted inside a tube of wood or iron slightly greater in diameter. Before the introduction of this type of rudder early in the 19th century, the front edge of the rudder was in a straight line from the tiller to the heel, so that when the rudder swung over the upper post or stock also swung over, necessitating a large hole under the counter and a large trunk inside the hull to give freedom of movement.

The hole under the counter for the gunstock rudder was made smaller than the trunk above it by having a light wooden ring nailed around it just clear of the rudder stock. To ship the rudder into place or remove it later, it had to be canted slightly for the gudgeons to clear each other, and therefore the opening under the counter had to be large enough to permit this, being afterwards enclosed by the wooden ring. A large ringbolt or a hole for it was fitted on the top edge of the rudder for lifting tackle, and often used for relieving tackle, led to eyebolts each side of the lower counter. The tackle was usually in the form of a chain pendant hanging in a loop each side of the rudder. Its purpose was to prevent the rudder being lost entirely if lifted off its pintles in heavy seas. It could also have rope tackles added to the chain to act as steering gear if the above deck steering gear became damaged. The later tea clippers omitted the relieving tackle from the rudder, although it was always kept aboard to rig in an emergency.

The mainpiece of the gunstock rudder formed the upper stock and was then cranked at an angle to become the middle of the rudder with additional pieces bolted to the fore and aft sides to form the body of the rudder, all held together by long bolts and tie braces. As the name implies, the complete unit resembled the stock of a rifle and its barrel, standing on end.

The rudder stock was of the same diameter as the top of the rudder and from there to the heel there was a slight tapering down to about two-thirds or half the stock diameter, which was also paralleled on the sternpost. The rudder blade also tapered slightly from its front to its aft edge.

The hinge apparatus consisted of braces and gudgeons on both the rudder and the sternpost with pintles linking the two, the pintles usually being removable pins. On small craft or those of earlier centuries, the pintles and rudder gudgeons were in one piece and were called rudder pintles and straps, those on the sternpost with the hole for the pin being called gudgeons. With the separate pintle, however, both parts were called gudgeons.

Because of the interaction of ferrous metal with copper sheathing and

RUDDERS

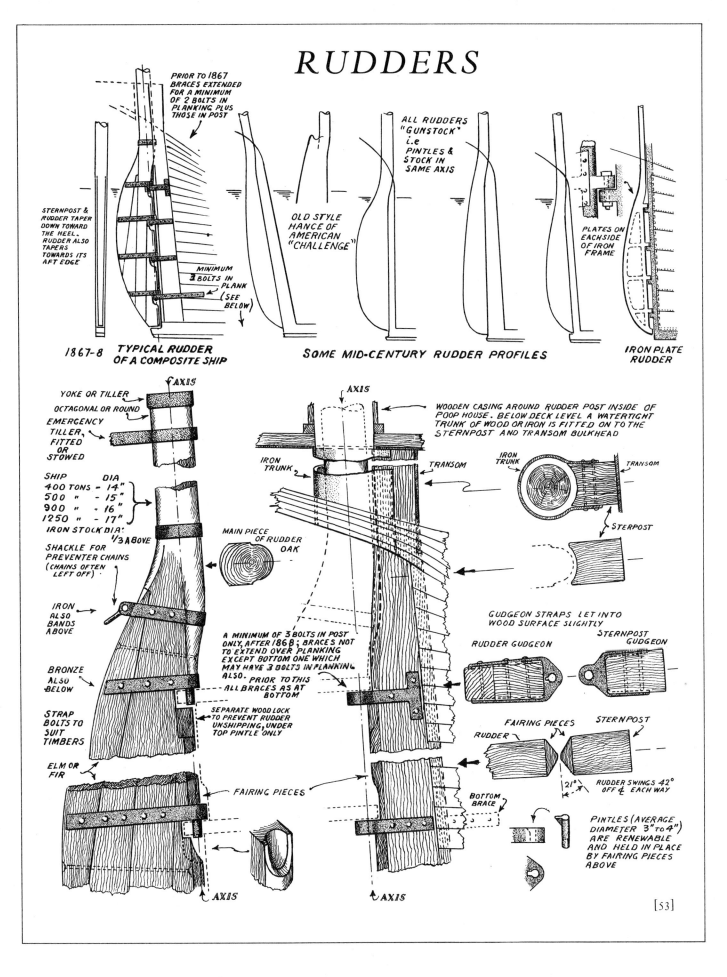

PRIOR TO 1867 BRACES EXTENDED FOR A MINIMUM OF 2 BOLTS IN PLANKING PLUS THOSE IN POST

STERNPOST & RUDDER TAPER DOWN TOWARD THE HEEL. RUDDER ALSO TAPERS TOWARDS ITS AFT EDGE

MINIMUM 3 BOLTS IN PLANK (SEE BELOW)

1867-8 TYPICAL RUDDER OF A COMPOSITE SHIP

ALL RUDDERS "GUNSTOCK" i.e PINTLES & STOCK IN SAME AXIS

OLD STYLE HANCE OF AMERICAN "CHALLENGE"

SOME MID-CENTURY RUDDER PROFILES

PLATES ON EACHSIDE OF IRON FRAME

IRON PLATE RUDDER

AXIS

YOKE OR TILLER
OCTAGONAL OR ROUND
EMERGENCY TILLER, FITTED OR STOWED

SHIP	DIA
400 TONS	14"
500 "	15"
900 "	16"
1250 "	17"

IRON STOCK DIA: 1/3 ABOVE

SHACKLE FOR PREVENTER CHAINS (CHAINS OFTEN LEFT OFF)

IRON ALSO BANDS ABOVE

BRONZE ALSO BELOW

STRAP BOLTS TO SUIT TIMBERS

ELM OR FIR

FAIRING PIECES

AXIS

AXIS

MAIN PIECE OF RUDDER OAK

IRON TRUNK

A MINIMUM OF 3 BOLTS IN POST ONLY, AFTER 1868; BRACES NOT TO EXTEND OVER PLANKING EXCEPT BOTTOM ONE WHICH MAY HAVE 3 BOLTS IN PLANKING ALSO. PRIOR TO THIS ALL BRACES AS AT BOTTOM

SEPARATE WOOD LOCK TO PREVENT RUDDER UNSHIPPING, UNDER TOP PINTLE ONLY

TRANSOM

BOTTOM BRACE

AXIS

WOODEN CASING AROUND RUDDER POST INSIDE OF POOP HOUSE. BELOW DECK LEVEL A WATERTIGHT TRUNK OF WOOD OR IRON IS FITTED ON TO THE STERNPOST AND TRANSOM BULKHEAD

IRON TRUNK

TRANSOM

STERPOST

GUDGEON STRAPS LET INTO WOOD SURFACE SLIGHTLY

RUDDER GUDGEON

STERNPOST GUDGEON

FAIRING PIECES

RUDDER

STERNPOST

21°

RUDDER SWINGS 42° OFF ₵ EACH WAY

PINTLES (AVERAGE DIAMETER 3" TO 4") ARE RENEWABLE AND HELD IN PLACE BY FAIRING PIECES ABOVE

[53]

fastenings, the gudgeons and pintles from the waterline down were made of bronze with the copper fitted neatly around them. Above the waterline the metalwork was frequently made of forged or wrought iron.

The braces were set at 90° to the axis of the pintles, and the arms or straps in the sternpost extended over some of the hull planking, sufficiently to take about two bolts in the upper and three in the lower in addition to three bolts in the sternpost. The heavy strain and sudden shocks on the rudder often caused leakage through the boltholes in the planking, and by the 1860s the braces were being made shorter so that all the bolts were contained in the sternpost. The upper strap was made in a tee shape to accommodate the three bolts if the post was narrow, although the lower one could extend onto the planking because its bolts were in the solid timber of the deadwood. This became a rule under Lloyd's in 1867 so all ships built to their rules after this date would have braces in this manner. This does not mean that vessels before 1867 did not have this arrangement, as it was frequently the case that a good shipbuilder would solve his own problems and Lloyd's would adopt the solution once it was proven. Some draughts of American ships in the early 1850s indicate short braces on the post. There were usually four sets of braces to the tea clipper of all sizes.

To prevent the rudder unshipping accidentally, the upper pintle had a woodlock nailed or screwed beneath it. This was a block of hardwood on the front of the rudder below the sternpost gudgeon which prevented the rudder from lifting. Rudders with the major width near the heel had slight buoyancy, being made of wood, and tended to lift if the stern was deeply immersed in a following sea. Fairing pieces were also nailed above the pintles on the front of the rudder to keep them in place.

The iron plated rudders conformed to similar contours to the wooden ones, but of course were much thinner. A basic wrought iron frame combined the stock and the gudgeons in one unit; some of the early ones had the pintles incorporated into the framework. Iron plates were riveted each side over the frame with the edges let in flush. The hollow spaces inside were filled with greenheart or oak chocks in pitch. The gudgeons on the stern frame were also incorporated into the frame, and the narrow confined space inside the hull in the deadwood area was filled in solid with a cement mix, as the riveting in this area was difficult and often defective.

Designers and builders had differing ideas about the best contours and areas for the rudder shape, some preferring the greatest width near the top, others in the middle, and some near the heel. This depended on where it was considered that the run of water following the lines of the hull was most effective and clear of eddies, especially with the vessel heeled.

The old fashioned type of hull with a heavy transom and a full shape near the waterline dragged a body of slack water behind it in which the rudder was not very effective, so that its maximum width was in the lower portion where there was a cleaner flow of water. This was the type of rudder seen on old naval draughts or those of East Indiamen, with the bottom almost square and then tapering upwards in a straight line with steps to the stock.

The advent of the fine-lined clippers saw the elimination of this square bottom and the introduction of a rounded heel and upper portion, the contour being half elliptical with its greatest width of body carried much higher, as there was a cleaner run of water behind the ship with a minimum of eddies. The rounded bottom to the rudder was also a protection if the ship grounded or touched her heel in shallow waters, and the slim tapered top above the waterline reduced the area liable to be struck by following or quartering seas.

The fullest width of rudder of the old pattern was approximately one-thirtieth of the ship's length, when the length was about four times the beam. As the length increased to five, six, or occasionally seven times the beam, the rudder width was based on a proportion of about one-eighth of the beam, which was the general average for a rudder shaped in an arc, as in the first example of drawing(53). In some cases the width was as little as one-tenth or one-eleventh of the beam, these types having much less curvature to the profile so as not to reduce the total area too much.

Sternposts on large ships had been made with a rake from earliest times for a number of reasons. It was easier to procure naturally grown shaped knees to connect the sternpost to the keelson if it was an obtuse angle rather than a right angle, a reason which was also influential in wooden ships being built with pronounced tumblehome at the deck levels for the sake of less angular beam knees. It was also found from long experience that a ship sailed better with a raking post as against a plumb one. The practice of moving weights aft to give trim by the stern also in effect increased the rake of the post.

The rudder was slightly more effective if raked, but required more power to operate even with the ship upright as it was hanging from the pintles by gravity, as against the upright post where the weight was directly borne in line with the pintles. Some designers also sought to gain slight advantage in the tonnage when the length of keel was used in the computation. By raking the post excessively they increased the deck length and retained the same tonnage as if the post had been vertical.

A well balanced ship was one in which the helmsman had little to do in all conditions of sailing, the chosen course being maintained by the balancing of the pressure on all sails against the lateral resistance of the hull. The centre of lateral resistance lay in a line approximately mid-length of the underwater profile, and the centre of effort of the sails theoretically with all sails set, up to 1/20 length aft of the CLR, but it could be moved forward or aft by varying the sails set at each extremity. The designer could also vary the centre of lateral resistance, which also included the rudder area, by rounding off the forefoot or altering the rake of the sternpost, thus reducing the deadwood area at each extremity as required. Too much deadwood such as in a sharp square forefoot resisted the turning action of a ship although it also helped to resist leeway.

The ultimate success of the balance, however, always rested with the master, who would study performance on each voyage until he understood the finer adjustments, and as the weather conditions worsened he could reduce sail progressively and still retain the balance without undue use of the helm. It required good perception, knowledge and intuition for success, and on taking over a new command a hitherto successful master could find himself with a ship which reacted quite differently from his previous experience. The action of the rudder is such that a resistance is set up on one side of the ship which in turn forces the ship to turn. Too frequent use of the rudder thus reduces the speed of the ship also, although obviously it is necessary to counteract the effect of heavy seas striking the bow or stern. This is all apart from the use of the rudder in inland waterways, rivers, docks, etc. where balance of sail does not help as the ship may be under tow or gliding to an anchor. The narrow rudder of the clipper ships was not very effective under these conditions and sometimes caused disasters such as those on the Min River from Foochow.

In describing the clipper ships from head to stern and their general construction and equipment, I have frequently used the expressions 'usually', 'typical', 'common to', 'often found' etc., which are somewhat indefinite. It is impossible to be precise on many points—the longer one investigates, the more one comes across some unusual variation.

Similarly, in commenting on the differences between American and British types, there are obviously cases where the difference is not very pronounced. There are many methods of framing a wooden hull, for instance, apart from the main systems described, and some could be common to both countries. Shipyard personnel in America were constantly being replenished with men from Europe who would continue to use their traditional skills and methods in many small ways which an experienced eye could detect, but I have endeavoured to take a comprehensive view of the more usual and obvious differences, such as would occasion a seaman to say on sighting a ship in dock or afloat 'She's an American' or 'She's British built', even though at times he might have been deceived.

Various mechanical appliances and fittings aboard a ship can be given a reasonably approximate date, based often on the date of the patent specification, but here again one cannot be precise in all cases. Some patented gear could be in existence for years before being generally accepted, and in other cases gear would be in use in some isolated instances before someone patented the idea.

Communication was not as widespread as one might suppose, especially regarding shipyards in isolated communities. I have found a surprising instance of this since World War II where a specification called for a wind deflector bulwark on a ship's bridge similar in pattern to that on the *Queen Mary* in the 1930s. The general manager of an excellent small British shipyard, who studied the specification, declared he had never heard of, or seen, such a thing. Research workers on early Royal Navy shipbuilding methods will sometimes come across an Admiralty order commanding a certain innovation to be made in construction, but quite often the innovation had already been made unofficially by some builders, and the Admiralty was merely confirming a successful idea.

Lloyd's in its early days did not issue a set of rules for construction, but instructed their surveyors to check the materials and workmanship against any known methods which were found from long experience to be bad. Gradually an accumulation of surveyors' reports enabled a reliable set of rules to be formulated, with strong emphasis on what should not be done, but this was a much slower process in the case of iron shipbuilding as builders were constantly innovating and improving, and were impatient with Lloyd's for not granting approval quickly enough, as has been mentioned in earlier chapters. But this caution was justified, and the

Chapter Sixteen

Conclusion

155

resulting rules became universally accepted standards which retained enough flexibility to consider and approve sensible variations.

Not all the more famous and admired ships were superior in workmanship, and some occasioned heavy repair bills to keep in operation. But when we look back to the era of the tea clippers, it is usually their physical appearance that arouses our interest and admiration, from photographs, prints, paintings or graphic descriptions. Exceptional speed and seaworthiness could be accomplished with less handsome and even ugly ships, arousing admiration of a different kind.

A handful of designers have had their names handed down to posterity; men who were highly skilled professionally, often as independent surveyors, who would be called in by a shipyard or shipowner to design a specific ship. But for the most part the individual creators of such beauty are unknown, although their shipyards are remembered.

Today much of what was wrought in these ships would be considered unnecessary and uneconomical, with our complete change in attitude toward life and the means of sustaining it. The ever-increasing pace impels us towards goals which some would consider are not yet proved to be the right ones, and many values which were satisfying ends in themselves have been lost on the way. The intense pride with which a seaman would sign on with the ship of his choice, despite the discomforts he knew were inevitable, is seldom met today, although its basis is still felt. I have spoken to stewards and seasoned passengers who would forgo the benefits of superior accommodation in a new ship for the sake of joining an older ship with a more handsome profile, whose photograph they would show with pride to their friends. A ship has to justify its existence economically, of course, but this is not the whole story. It is in itself an important part of the grand spectacle of life, showing itself to many people in strange lands at regular intervals, unlike the static structure of domestic architecture or civil engineering which has to be visited or sought out by possible admirers. The lower hull and bottom, the most intriguing and satisfying parts of a ship to the eye, are unfortunately only seen in drydock by those intimately connected with their operation. The subtle and sensuous sweeps and bends which are also entirely functional defy those whose arguments would seem to blur the difference between beauty and ugliness.

The delightful form of the hull of a tea clipper, gently twisting from a hollowed curve and flare at the bows to a slight inward inclination or tumblehome and then reversing the twist again into the grand sweep under the counter stern, all being moulded perfectly into the curves toward the keel, must surely rank as the most aesthetically perfect manmade shape. There is much to be learned about the purpose of life in looking back—as in our regard of the tea clipper.